Breaths from Beyond the Curtain

Spiritual Guidance of the Naqshbandi Sufi Masters

By

Shaykh Nazim Adil Al-Haqqani

Foreword By

Shaykh Muhammad Hisham Kabbani

Institute for Spiritual and Cultural Advancement

© Copyright 2010 Institute for Spiritual and Cultural Advancement.

All rights reserved. No part of this book may be reproduced, stored in a retrieval system, or transmitted in any form, or by any means, electronic, mechanical, photocopying, or otherwise, without the written permission of the Institute for Spiritual and Cultural Advancement.

Library of Congress Cataloging-in-Publication Data

TBD

Published and Distributed by:

Institute for Spiritual and Cultural Advancement

17195 Silver Parkway, #401
Fenton, MI 48430 USA
Tel: (888) 278-6624
Fax:(810) 815-0518
Email: staff@naqshbandi.org
Web: http://www.naqshbandi.org

First Edition June 2010
ISBN: 978-1-930409-81-1

Author Mawlana Shaykh Muhammad Nazim Adil al-Haqqani, world leader of the Most Distinguished Naqshbandi-Haqqani Sufi Order.

CONTENTS

About Shaykh Nazim	viii
Foreword	xvii
Introduction	xix
Publisher's Note	xxiii
Notes	xxiv
The Importance of Beginning with God's Name	2
The Emptiness of Material Satisfactions	12
Concerning Ego Control	19
Concerning Harmful Freedom	28
The Critical Need for a Global Change	39
Choosing Acceptable, Right Actions	45
Today's "Top Point of Civilization"	51
Living Breaths and Poisoned Breaths	61
Concerning Men and Women	68
Concerning Pregnancy, Childbirth and Nursing	77
Pride Is Only for Allah	85
Consider Yourself To Be Nothing	93
Our Stolen Diamonds	102
Seeking Limitless Levels in the Divine Presence	109
About Being Truth Defenders	116
Regarding the State of the Muslim World	126
"O Mankind, You Have Been Honoured!"	137
The Ottoman Islamic Legacy	142
Knowing Yourself	149
Keeping Islamic Orders	156
Seeking Knowledge That Benefits	162
The Necessity of Believing in the Last Messenger	169
Opening Our Hearts to Heavenly Lights Through Faith	177
Imagination Versus Reality	182

All Things Change Except Allah *Ta'ala* 189
Concerning Black Holes 195
Concerning the Need for a Trainer and Guide 201
Humankind Wants to Reach Somewhere 209
The Importance of Seeking Spiritual Perfection 215
The Real Goal of the Naqshbandi *Tariqah* 222
Material Aspects Never Give Satisfaction 228
Glossary 235

About Shaykh Nazim

I had been fortunate enough to accompany the Shaykh together with his son-in-law, Shaykh Hisham Kabbani, in the United States in 1998 for a period of three weeks. During this time we toured New York, visited the United Nations and met with politicians on Capitol Hill in Washington.

Also part of the entourage were the muftis of Albania and Kosovo as well as the [late] Chechen president, Aslan Maskhadov. These activities were the precursor to the 2nd International Conference of the Islamic Supreme Council of America in Washington.

As the resident photographer I was privileged to witness first-hand something of the essence of the fortieth Grand Shaykh of the Naqshbandi Sufi order, an order that traces its lineage back in a "golden chain" to the Prophet Muhammad ☻ through his greatest companion Abu Bakr as-Siddiq ☬.

In 1998 I wrote that Shaykh Nazim was a spiritual colossus of the twentieth century. And while his contribution to the inner peace of humanity will never win him a Nobel Prize, it has to be remembered that at least half a million people have embraced Islam at his feet.

His *murids* (or followers) are said to run into millions and include heads of state, pop stars, and even allegedly Prince Charles. In that regard, I once heard Shaykh Nazim say that he was a collector of souls.

Of this I have no doubt, as in America I saw non-Muslims become mesmerised by his spiritual luminosity. In one instance I remember a crack junkie becoming a Muslim after meeting the Shaykh for two hours and in another, a CNN journalist saying *shahada* (Islam's testification of faith) after hearing him speak.

I saw complete strangers take his hand in the foyer of the United Nations, in the streets of New York and in the tree-lined avenues of Capitol Hill.

But in spite of all this, Shaykh Nazim remained down-to-earth, humble, sweet natured and loving to all. A pauper was treated as equally as a prince was in his company, and I never saw him ever turn anyone away.

His recent visit to Cape Town, South Africa, typified all of this. Whether playfully beating video man Dawood Schroeder with his stick on Table Mountain, bantering with tourists, or conversing with the late Shaykh Nazim Mohamed at the Muslim Judicial Council, he was always at the same time serious, witty and incredibly insightful.

His apparently simple *sohbets* or talks were often exactly the opposite, deep, cryptic, metaphysical - and extremely challenging. I mean, for example, how many '*alims* can explain ibn 'Arabi's *wahdat al-wujud* (the unity of being) in three sentences?

After witnessing him in action for a week in Cape Town, my feelings about Shaykh Nazim have been reconfirmed. Yes, he is definitely a spiritual giant of our times. But in so saying, describing him has become even more difficult! …

As a multi-layered personality, Shaykh Nazim is many things to many people. In his presence, one feels strangely secure. He is definitely the kind of person you would like to share a bomb shelter with.

As a person who treads lightly in the *dunya* he may appear soft and bending (like the proverb of the Malaysian rice plant in the wind) but when it comes to submitting to his Creator, he is unwavering. Here, it is easy to sense that his iman is like steel.

Perhaps the uniqueness of Shaykh Nazim in this arrogant day and age is his manner of approach. His presence does not announce itself to you as king or conqueror but rather as a servant. What is so engaging is that he essentially humbles himself to you with a fine-tuned subtlety before you realise that you must humble yourself to him.

One of his favourite English expressions is "Mercy Oceans," his Grand Shaykh 'Abdullah ad-Daghestani's way of explaining the Sunnah and its countless mercies. And for those who think the Sunnah—the way of our beloved master Muhammad ﷺ —is a simple matter of beard length and counting the rewards like bank notes, there is a very rude awakening.

For Shaykh Nazim the Sunnah is strict Shari'ah—as well as charity, generosity, hard work, heart knowledge and compassion.

Of all the people I have encountered on this earth, Sayyid Mawlana Shaykh Nazim Adil al-Haqqani is the closest I have seen anybody come to epitomise the Sunnah. In his commanding presence I felt like an unclean grain of sand being washed around in the depths of his "Mercy Oceans."

I remember him once saying on the lawn of a *murid*'s house: "My people, are you happy? Allah is happy. The Angels are happy. They are not for crying..." Indeed, in just a few words he had taught us the excellence of a positive outlook on life and the fact that other people's hearts will open like flowers to a smile.

But on a deeper level with these simple words he had actually taught the real lesson, the *adab* of viceregency.

In another instance he said that man was chasing zeroes. "Are you going to show your checkbook to Allah?" he asked with a chuckle. "The aim of mankind today is to collect zeroes, but you have been created for Allah's divine service. Service for *dunya* is not for Allah Almighty..."

After being rudely challenged from the floor in a Cape Town mosque and accused of contravening the Sunnah, Shaykh Nazim came up with the following *sohbet* a few hours later.

"Rasulullah ﷺ[1] called people to him, he was a saviour of souls. Some came to him saying 'save our souls' and he saved them as they surrendered. These (pious) people were respected whether living or dead. Shaytan became angry because of this...

"Shaytan becomes angry if a saved person is (particularly) from the sahabis or the *awliya*. Shaytan wants these people to be taken away. He is the biggest enemy of the pious. People destroy tombs and *mazars* of the *awliya* because

---

[1] ﷺ stands for *"Salla-Lahu 'alayhi wa sallam,"* meaning, "Allah's peace and blessings be upon him," the Islamic invocation for Prophet Muhammad ﷺ.

Shaytan asks for them not to be known. He wants the ummah to forget them...that's the reason for no tombstones!

"Allah says don't forget people who did their best for Me, these people who gave their souls for Islam, but Shaytan wants them to be forgotten. Shaytan wants his people to destroy everything that was against Shaytan. Shaytan is crying for his hatred..Shaytan (is jealous of good) and wants to destroy the graves of those who killed Abu Jahl..."

It was a devastating critique of the Salafis but no less a serious warning directed at our very own *nafs*.

I could go on forever quoting Shaykh Nazim's pearls of wisdom dropped into the "Mercy Oceans" net for the seeker throughout the day. In nearly a month of observing his behaviour I have never seen him talk from notes. He sleeps little and his day starts well before Fajr (dawn) and often ends in the early hours of the morning.

For those who challenge the credentials of Shaykh Nazim it is perhaps best to remember that he is an orthodox Sunni Muslim down to his fingertips and studied Shari'ah, Qur'anic sciences and Hadith under great masters in Turkey, Syria and the Lebanon.

He is the mufti of Turkish Cyprus and is an acknowledged *'alim* of Hanafi *fiqh*, apart from possessing a Masters Degree in Chemical Engineering from Istanbul University.

Academic qualifications aside, Shaykh Nazim is a Sayyid (a descendent of the Holy Prophet ﷺ) on both the Hasani and Husayni lines. Through his father he traces his lineage back to Sayyid 'Abdul Qadir Jilani ؓ (the great 10th century saint) and through his mother to Mawlana Jalaluddin Rumi ؓ.

As a Grand-Shaykh of the Naqshbandi tariqat Shaykh Nazim also carries *ijazah* (permission to teach) in other orders such as the Qadiri and Rifa'i'.

Physically, Shaykh Nazim is small of stature but somehow seems to be much taller than he actually is. He may well be past his 80th year, but when he strides out (his walking stick before him like an *alif*), it's always as if one is trying to keep up with him. I have also never seen him miss his *salat*, even when on travel... He has performed the Hajj 27 times, has undergone rigorous spiritual seclusion on many occasions and has established Islamic centres around the world.

Indeed, the *baraka* of Shaykh Nazim spreads wherever he travels. Cape Town was no exception. A person I know was embraced by the Shaykh and shortly afterwards dreamt of Sayyidina Abu Bakr ﷺ. Another who had not met Shaykh Nazim or any of his entourage was given advice in a dream by one of his *khalifas* (Shaykh Hisham).

A moment on his last night in a country mosque outside Cape Town will stay in the memory for a long time. Shaykh Nazim had asked the question: "What goodness has the modern (university) graduate brought to society without the Holy Books?" After suggesting that "Tariqat says keep Sunnah, the essence of Shari'ah," he then went on to talk about the threat of secularism.

"Oh my people, 20th century education is aimed at bringing people to the level of animals...higher education is not leading to Allah when the name of Allah is prohibited," he said.

"We are living in a time that truth is lost and defenders of truth have disappeared...I ask for you to be defenders of truth."

The "Oh my people" rang like a bell. "Oh my ummah!" At that moment it seemed as if it was not Shaykh Nazim talking, but the Prophet ﷺ. Shaykh Nazim had become the Sunnah! Great men, friends of Allah, who see with the eyes of Allah and whose hearts beat with the unison of the *kalimah*, enjoy vision through the agency of the Prophet ﷺ.

Perhaps, in conclusion, it would be fitting to recall something remarkably profound that Shaykh Nazim uttered on top of Table Mountain, an event that lent itself to much symbolism. Before that the Shaykh had "communed" with nature, admiring the view of the city and ocean 1,000 metres below and playfully eying a rock rabbit.

As Hafiz Mahmoud Sahib made the *adhan* for Dhuhr, a bird on a ledge before him sang its heart out. After making Dhuhr *salat* on one of the viewing platforms that faced north from the southernmost city of Africa, he turned around and then challenged those in Cape Town who had been attacking him but who had declined to confront him in debate.

"They come here, we all jump together, and then we see who floats," he said, ominously waving his hand like a butterfly settling on a flower.

Shafiq Morton
Cape Town, South Africa
November, 2000

Copyright al-Qalam Magazine

SHAYKH NAZIM ADIL AL-HAQQANI

FOREWORD

Bismillahi-r-Rahmani-r-Raheem
In the Name of God, the Most Beneficent, the Most Merciful

All praise is due to God Almighty, Allah the Exalted and Bounteous and the most fluent, abundant and sweet praise and blessings be upon His perfect servant, the mercy to all creation and exemplar of perfect character, ethics and morality Prophet Muhammad ﷺ, and upon his family and Companions.

This book is a compendium of *sohbets* or spiritual discourses by our master—chief of saints and reviver of the Prophetic path to divine enlightenment, teacher of millions and worldwide leader of the Naqshbandi-Haqqani Sufi Order, Mawlana Shaykh Muhammad Nazim Adil al-Haqqani, may Allah grant him health and long life.

It is related that in the Last Days of this world—which, based upon the predicted indications is taking place even as I pen these words—those who adhere to the pure teachings of the prophets and saints will become rare. On the contrary, those who breach the Prophetic Tradition, the Sunnah, will be commonplace.

No prior prophet ever mentioned in such detail what Prophet Muhammad ﷺ foretold fourteen hundred years ago. In the seventh century, he gave a precise description with specific details which were not fully understood until their manifestation in the present age. The Prophet ﷺ explained what would transpire in the Last Days so that the people witnessing those events could recognize their place in time. The Prophet ﷺ warned that when bedouin Arabs compete to construct lofty buildings in the desert the Hour of Judgment would be close. He predicted that in the Last Days, trustworthy people would be vilified regarded as traitors by the people.

In a Prophetic Tradition[2] it is related that a bedouin came to Prophet Muhammad ﷺ and asked when Judgment Day would take place. He said, "When the trust (*al-amana*) is lost, then await Judgment Day." The bedouin asked, "How will it be lost?" The Prophet ﷺ replied, "When power and authority comes in the hands of unfit persons, then wait for the Judgment Day."[3] He also has said that "the trustworthy one will be called a traitor."

As the Prophet ﷺ predicted, the psychology of people in our time is the opposite of what is prescribed and it is nearly impossible to find a trustworthy person. At the same time, everywhere on earth, different groups are busy destroying what remains of faith and spirituality, each one following its own agenda. Even "spiritual" groups and individuals slander each other, and through their corrupt behavior, support falsehood—all the while claiming to be believers.

The words of the tradition, "The trustworthy, *al-amin*, one will be said to be a traitor," has an interpretation. Al-Amin is one of the names of Prophet Muhammad ﷺ, and one of the signs of the Last Days is that people will attack the Prophets of God, in particular the Last Messenger, Mu-

---

[2] Arabic: *hadith*.
[3] Sahih Bukhari.

hammad ﷺ, and the message he brought for mankind's felicity.

Alhamdulillah—praise God—we are fortunate to be students or disciples of Mawlana Shaykh Nazim. As long as he, and Sufi masters like him, continue to teach the ways of the the prophets and saints, hope remains for humankind. For his teachings, while outwardly plain, are endowed with a wisdom and grace seldom found today. The shaykh's words take you back to a simpler time, when people were straightforward, when they what they meant, and when they did what they said.

May God bless you as you pick up this volume and read some of the holy teachings he has brought. It is well known in the Naqshbandi Sufi tradition, that pure words of guidance are able to elevate the reader to the stations and states described simply through the blessed character, *baraka*, of one authorized to teach them. Futher, these teachings will remain with you and part of you in this life and on, into the hereafter.

I am only a student and I have been learning from my teacher Mawlana Shaykh Nazim, who, despite his 85 years of age is still incredibly active spreading the teachings that come to his heart from the spiritual "central headquarters." What I saw and learned from my master I cannot express because those fountains are always pouring forth, continuously flowing. The hearts of such saints are like waterfalls: giving always and they are not asking to take anything, asking only to give.

As the world around us seems to slide further into its darkest chapter, in a time when negativity and skepticism insistently challenge faith, the faithful of all beliefs seek a beacon that will lead them to a divine shelter of peace and protection. Presented in this volume are essential aspects of a spiritual discipline which dates back to the time when Prophet Muhammad delivered the divine message—a message preserved by Sufi masters over forty generations.

In these times when Islam is more and more visible on the world stage, it is hoped through this humble work that readers will come to better understand the true teachings of Islam, namely, the universal endorsement to practice moderation and follow the middle course, to hold patience, to uphold tolerance and respect for others, to approach conflict resolution in peaceful ways, to condemn all forms of terrorism, and above all, to love God, appreciate His Divine favors, and strive in His divine service. The greatest Islamic teaching is that there is no higher station than to serve the Lord Almighty.

Shaykh Muhammad Hisham Kabbani
Fenton, Michigan
October 28, 2007

INTRODUCTION

Endless praise and thanks be to God Most High, who guides His servants to His light by means of other servants of His whose hearts He illuminates with His divine love.

Since the beginning of human history, God Most High has conveyed His revealed guidance to mankind through His prophets and messengers, beginning with the first man, Adam ﷺ. The prophetic line includes such well-known names as Noah, Abraham, Ishmael, Isaac, Jacob, Joseph, Lot, Moses, David, Solomon, and Jesus, peace be upon them all, ending and culminating in Muhammad, the Seal of the Prophets ﷺ, a descendant of Abraham ﷺ, who brought the final revelation from God to all mankind.

But although there are no longer prophets upon the earth, the Most Merciful Lord has not left His servants without inspired teachers and guides. *Awliya*—holy people or saints—are the inheritors of the prophets. Up to the Last Day, these "friends of God," the radiant beacons of truth, righteousness and the highest spirituality, will continue in the footsteps of the prophets, calling people to their Lord and guiding seekers to His glorious Divine Presence.

One such inspired teacher, a shaykh or *murshid* of the Naqshbandi Sufi Order, is Shaykh Nazim Adil al-Qubrusi al-Haqqani. A descendant not only of the Holy Prophet Muhammad ﷺ but also of the great Sufi masters 'Abul Qadir Gilani and Jalaluddin Rumi, Shaykh Nazim was born in Larnaca, Cyprus, in 1922 during the period of British rule of the island. Gifted from earliest childhood with an extraordinarily spiritual personality, Shaykh Nazim received his spiritual training in Damascus at the hands of Mawlana Shaykh 'Abdullah ad-Daghestani (fondly referred to as "Grandshaykh"), the mentor of such well-known figures as Gurjieff and J. G. Bennett, over a period of forty years.

Before leaving this life in 1973, Grandshaykh designated Shaykh Nazim as his successor. In 1974, Shaykh Nazim went to London for the first time, thus initiating what was to become a yearly practice during the month of Ramadan up to 1990s. A small circle of followers began to grow around him, eagerly taking their training in the ways of Islam and *tariqah* at his hands.

From this humble beginning, the circle has grown to include thousands of *murids* or disciples in various countries of the world, among whom are to be found many eminent individuals, both religious and secular. Shaykh Nazim is a luminous, tremendously impressive spiritual personality, radiating love, compassion and goodness. He is regarded by many of his *murids* as the *qutub* or chief saint of this time.

The shaykh teaches through a subtle interweaving of personal example and talks ("Associations" or *sohbets*), invariably delivered extempore according to the inspirations that are given to him. He does not lecture, but rather pours out from his heart into the hearts of his listeners such knowledge and wisdoms as may change their innermost beings and bring them toward their Lord as His humble, willing, loving servants.

Shaykh Nazim's language and style are unique, so eloquent, moving and flavorful that not only do his teachings seem inspired but also his extraordinary use of words. His *sohbets* represent the teachings of a twentieth century Sufi master, firmly grounded in Islamic orthodoxy, speaking to the hearts of the seekers of God of any faith tradition from his own great, wide heart, in a tremendous outpouring of truth, wisdom and divine knowledge which is surely unparalleled in the English language, guiding the seeker toward the Divine Presence.

The sum total of Shaykh Nazim's message is that of hope, love, mercy and reassurance. In a troubled and uncertain world in which old, time-honored values have given place to new ones of confused origins and unclear prospects, in which a feeling heart and thinking mind is constantly troubled by a sense of things being terribly disordered and out of control, in which the future seems forebodingly dark and uncertain for humanity, he proclaims God's love and care for His servants, and invites them to give their hearts to Him.

Shaykh Nazim holds out to seekers the assurance that even their smallest steps toward their Lord will not go unnoticed and unresponded to. Rather than threatening sinners with the prospect of eternal Hell, he offers hope of salvation from the Most Merciful Lord, and heart-warming encouragement and incentive for inner change and growth. As one who has traversed every step of the seeker's path and reached its pinnacle, he offers both inner and practical guidelines for attaining the highest spiritual goals.

The talks in this book were given in spring 2004, at Mawlana's home in Cyprus. Each of these talks is entirely extempore, as Shaykh Nazim never prepares his words but invariably speaks according to inspirations coming to his heart.

In keeping with the shaykh's methodology—the methodology of the prophets, particularly of the Last Prophet, Muhammad, peace be upon him and upon them all, and of the Qur'an itself—of reinforcing vital lessons by repetition and reiteration, the same themes and anecdotes recur again and again. The talks seem to come in unannounced clusters, centering around a primary theme, which develops and evolves according to the spiritual state of the listeners. Thus, Shaykh Nazim may cite the same verse or *hadith*, or tell the same tale on different occasions, each time reinforcing a slightly different aspect of the eternal message of love and light which is Islam.

The shaykh's talks are interspersed with words and phrases from Arabic and other Islamic languages. These are translated either in the text itself, in footnotes the first time they occur, or, for general and recurrent terms, in the Glossary at the end of this volume. Qur'anic verses quoted in the text have been referenced for easy access.

Every attempt has been made to retain the shaykh's original language with minimal editing. However, since these talks were transcribed from audio tapes recorded on amateur equipment by listeners for their own personal use (or, in the case this volume, by a *murid* extremely familiar with the shaykh's language and ideas, by hand), some inadvertent errors may have found their way into the text. For these, we ask Allah's forgiveness and your kind indulgence. May He fill your heart with light and love as you read and reflect upon these inspired words, and guide you safely to His exalted Divine Presence.

Publisher's Note

Shaykh Nazim is fluent in Arabic, Turkish and Greek, and semi-fluent in Engish. Over three decades, his llectures have been transated into twenty or more languages, and to date have reached the furthest corners of the globe. We sincerely hope the reader will appreciate the author's unique language style, which has been painstakingly preserved in this work.

As some of the terms in this book may be foreign, to assist the reader we have provded transliterations, as well as a detailed glossary.

NOTES

The following symbols are universally recognized and have been respectfully included in this work:

The symbol ﷺ represents *sall-Allahu 'alayhi wa sallam* (Allah's blessings and greetings of peace be upon him), which is customarily recited after reading or pronouncing the holy name of Prophet Muhammad ﷺ.

The symbol ؑ represents *'alayhi 's-salam* (peace be upon him/her), which is customarily recited after reading or pronouncing the holy names of the other prophets, family members of Prophet Muhammad ﷺ, the pure and virtuous women in Islam, and the angels.

The symbol ؓ/ؓ represents *radi-Allahu 'anhu/'anha* (may Allah be pleased with him/her), which is customarily recited after reading or pronouncing the holy names of Companions of the Prophet ﷺ.

In the Name of Allah, The Beneficent and The Munificent

This, my English, is strange English. Not everyone can understand because, *subhanallah*, meanings are coming to my heart, and when running in my heart to give to you, I am using any means – from here, from there - bringing any word which may be useful.

I am like a person waiting for water to run out from the faucet. Then, when suddenly it comes, and he knows the water is going to be turned off, stop running, he may take any container – with a no-good shape, broken on one side, or anything he may find there – quickly bringing them to take that water and store it. Therefore, when meanings are coming to my heart, I am trying to explain with any word, which you may understand or not. But you must understand, because we have a saying, "Listeners must be more wise than speakers." Therefore, when inspiration comes, we must explain.

They are living words, not plastic – bananas, plastic; apples, plastic, and grapes. Even if the shapes are not much, they are living, real. When you are going to arrange them in measures, good system; when you are going to be engaged by outside forms, you are losing meanings. ▲

1

THE IMPORTANCE OF BEGINNING WITH GOD'S NAME

A'udhu bil-Lahi min ash-Shaytani-r-rajeem. Bismillahi-r-Rahmani-r-Raheem. La hawla wa la quwwata illa bil-Lahi-l-'Aliyi-l-'Azheem.

Without saying Allah's Holy Name, everything that you are doing is rubbish and will be thrown away as unacceptable.

When Allah Almighty created *al-Qalam*, the Pen,[1] He first looked at it, and from the greatness of Allah Almighty's looking, that pen was split, a cleft coming (in old-time pens, there was always a cleft at the end of the pen) And Allah Almighty ordered the Pen, the holy Pen, the first Pen, saying, "Write!"

All things hear His holy command. All things have senses. Without senses, nothing is in existence—hearing and answering and glorifying; hearing and listening and obeying and glorifying, everything in existence. Even though we say that rocks have no life, no speaking, no look-

---

[1] The celestial Pen that writes the destinies of all things in creation on *al-Lawh al-Mahfuzh*, the Preserved Tablet of Allah's decrees for all eternity.

ing, no answering—no. It is so to you. That is the level of creatures. For creatures, everything, is within limits, but for the Creator, they must hear, they must listen, they must obey, they must give their service, and their service is to glorify their Creator. Atoms, or smaller particles that come together and become atoms, each small particle, also, must hear because He, Almighty, is calling them. When He says, "Come into existence!" they come; when ordering, "Stay here," staying there; "Listen to Me," listening; "Be obedient to Me," being obedient; "Glorify Me," glorifying.

Only heedless mankind do not look at that point, so *jahil*, so ignorant. *"Innahu kana dhaluman jahula."*[2] The Lord of Heavens is mentioning the characteristic of mankind, *"jahula"*—the most ignorant ones in existence, who have been created to be patrons and deputies on earth over every creation, but they are so ignorant that there is no scale for measuring their ignorance. And in particular, they have reached the final limit of ignorance in our days, in the twenty-first century.

I am speaking according to the western calendar, because they are unbelievers. If they were believers, they would have given their respect to the Seal of the Prophets ﷺ, the honour of creation; but instead, they followed their imagination, and that calendar by which they are calling this year 2004 is just built on such fancies. The real calendar that began with the emigration of the Seal of Prophets, peace be upon him and upon every prophet, is a fixed calendar.[3] No

---

[2] *"He [man] was unjust and ignorant."* (33:72)
[3] The Islamic *(Hijri)* calendar is a lunar calendar corresponding to the sighting of each month's new moon. This calendar began with the emi-

one can have any doubt that now it is the year 1424. And after one-and-half months it is going to be 1425.

There is no doubt about the Islamic calendar's beginning. But Shaytan is making unbelievers, non-Muslims, not care about their calendar. And heedless Muslims, also, no-mind, no-honour Muslims, they are printing the non-Muslims calendar, together with only a few brief words about the most honoured one's, Sayyidina Muhammad's calendar, the Islamic calendar. Sadly, our nation has also joined those heedless people, no one coming and saying, "Why are we not using *our* calendar, the Islamic calendar?"

Why? What is the honour of their calendar, the non-Muslim calendar? If the Islamic world uses the non-Muslim calendar, will westerners put crowns on Muslims? No. They are saying about Muslims, "They are our tails. We are heads and they are our tails." No value for Muslims in the sight of Western people, the non-Muslim world. It is blameworthy for Muslims. Therefore, Muslims are in the worst situation now. We must be obedient to Allah in everything!

As we are saying now, mankind is claiming that they reached the final limit of their civilization, or they are thinking that they reached the top point of technology and that there is nothing beyond that technology for man to reach. "And we are representing it," Western people are saying about their technology.

---

gration of the Prophet ﷺ from Mecca to Medina in the year 62 C.E. (622 C.E.).

And technology is nothing; material powers are nothing, compared to spiritual power. Technology may change. In one second, only one person who is authorized by spiritual power may remove all the world's technology. No need for another second; in only one second it may finish. But They[4] are not using their power, They are not looking at this dirty life, *dunya daniya*,[5] which means the lowest life for creatures. But people are saying, "High life, the highest!" And heedless Muslims are following them.

Yesterday there was an accident, a plane falling down. What did their technology do? Why wasn't it protecting it? But if one person, an authorized, spiritually powerful person, were to look from here and say, "Don't fall down! Continue on your way," that plane must hear and must obey. Technology can't do that. It is under the hegemony of material aspects; it can't do anything contrary to natural laws. But spiritual people have been authorized by Heavens. They may do as they like, but your technology can't do as *you* like.

Yes. The most disobedient, most unbelieving people are now living on earth, and such a punishment is coming on them that, if you collected all the punishments that passed away from the beginning up to today, they would be nothing compared to the punishment those foolish people should receive, because they are making themselves like

---

[4]As noted previously, "They" refers to *awliya*, the holy people or saints of Islam.

[5]Arabic: *dunya daniya*, this low/ base/despicable world.

Pharaoh or Nimrod.⁶ They are claiming that they are creators, *astagfirullah!*⁷ Only the Lord creates!

When Allah Almighty ordered the holy Pen, "Write," it said, "O my Lord, what is Your order to be written on the Preserved Tablet?"

He, Almighty, was saying, in His greatness, "Write My Holy Names. Write *'Bismillahi-r-Rahmani-r-Raheem.'*" And the Pen wrote. Our traditional knowledge that comes from Heavens informs us that, at the time (where 'time' is just for our understanding) the holy Pen wrote, "*Bismillahi-r-Ruhmuni r Raheem*," It took seven hundred years like our years to write it. "And under that, write everything that is going to be now and in the future up to the end, up to the Day of Resurrection." And it was written.

That is a powerful point, and it is holy knowledge by which Allah Almighty wants to teach His servants not to be heedless. Everything that is under the *'unwan*, heading, of "*Bismillahi-r-Rahmani-r-Raheem,*" is an honoured action and that phrase gives honour to the one who does that action. The reward that you should be granted, it is only for those actions that are headed or crowned by "*Bismillahi-r-Rahmani-r-Raheem.*" If not, such action is rubbish. Throw it away in the dustbin!

---

⁶Nimrod and the pharaoh of Moses are mentioned in the Qur'an as prototypes of arrogant, oppressive unbelievers with temporary ranks of worldly power.

⁷Arabic: *astagfirullah*, I seek Allah's forgiveness.

Subhanallah, glory be to Allah Almighty! There is a city in England, Halifax, and they weave this famous *kashmir*, cashmere, there in factories. Then a supervisor comes and does a control on it for flaws, defects. People will not accept a flaw; they want pure, perfect cashmere, without flaws in it. And for each *ma'moul*, product, employees are looking and saying "We can't give this to customers. They will say, 'No, this is not good,' and it is going to be blame on our factory. We must look, we must take care."

They are taking so much care for such a thing. Then do you think that angels do not look at your actions? Looking—"Is there *'Bismillah'*?"

"No *'Bismillah.'*"

"Throw it away, throw it away, throw it away!" For twenty-four hours that person is working, working, but Allah's great Names—honoured, honourable, glorious Names—are not there, and *malayka*, angels, are saying, "Away, away, away!" And no value and no honour for those people who are working and not mentioning their Lord and Creator's holy Names. *Allahu Akbar!*

That is the essence of the global crisis, not economics; no. They have lost their honour. Mankind now are doing everything for Shaytan, not for Allah. If they were doing for Allah, *dunya* would quickly change to be Paradise—no troubles, no problems, no sufferings, no enmity, no envy. Everyone would be in perfection because of the holy command to the earth, "Look at My servants' actions. If they are living for Me, if they are doing for Me, if they are concerned about Me, be Paradise for them so their lives will be like in Paradise"—not the Paradise that will be in eternity, but in a state that is going to be like Paradise.[8] But they have forgotten their Creator.

I am looking at the full moon. Since some time, perhaps from the beginning of this holy month, I am looking, particularly as people are thinking that they will send something to Mars. From far away, Mars is seen as a globe. And I am looking at the moon, also. It is, in the darkness of space, also a shining global *jism*, a global object.

I am thinking: They are saying that [from space] they are seeing our planet, this world, also as a globe. I am looking and saying, "*Subhanallah!* Those foolish, materialist people, those who have no belief, why do they not look and think?" And I am asking them now, "If there is no Creator, how and from where do you think these people that are on this planet came? How can they have been on this globe—*how?*

"If no one brought them to it and they came here by themselves, how can this world be, as Allah Almighty says, '*Fil-fulki-l-mashun*'?[9] Other heavenly bodies are like empty vessels, but our planet is full of countless kinds of creatures; those planets, no. How, from where, did they come, these people on this planet?"

They are never thinking about it, how it can be!

And concerning those people who think that they reached Mars and are asking about life on it, Allah Al-

---

[8]Cf., Qur'an 7:96: *"If only the people of the cities had believed and feared Allah, We would have opened to them blessings from the heaven and earth...."*
[9]*"The laden ship"* [Noah's ark]. (36:41)

mighty is saying, *"Wa ja'alna mina-l-ma'i kulla shayin hayy."*[10] The Lord of the universe, the Lord of Heavens, is saying, "I made every living creature from water." Without water, no life. That One who created water from hydrogen and oxygen, making a marriage between two hydrogen atoms and one oxygen atom, making water, is saying, "And from that I gave you life on this planet."

Those planets at which you are looking are dry. But they [atheists and skeptics] are against holy books, always. They can't pass beyond what is put in front of you as a limit, no; they want to pass but they can't pass. Allah Almighty is saying, "I give life from water." And they are looking [at Mars' surface] and saying, "It is sand."[11]

So many times they tried the moon, to see if there are some creatures. I am saying, "When you land on it, the creatures are hiding themselves." [Mawlana laughs.] They are hiding themselves by command of the Qutbu-l mutasarrif.[12]

On every planet there is life, but not life like on this planet, our planet, no. It has a special existence. For others, Allah Almighty's Power Oceans can't be within limits. *Li*

---

[10] *"And We made every living thing from water."* (21:30)

[11] That is, although Allah says that He created every living thing from water, people are nonetheless expecting to find life as we know it on a dry planet like Mars.

[12] *Qutb*—pole saint, leader of of all saints; the saint who represents the Prophet at any time who is head of four other *qutbs*, each with a special area of responsibility. They are: Qutb, Qutbu-l Aqtab, Qutbu-l Bilad, Qutbu-l Irshad, Qutbu-l Mutassarif. Qutbu-l-mutasarrif is the pole saint who manages all happenings in this world, through God's creatures.

kulli makan makin.[13] If He created that place, there must be some creatures in it; but Allah Almighty is not confined, never going to be under any natural laws forcing Him to do this—no. He is free to do anything, everything. He created that planet. There must be on it so many creatures, but you can't see, you can't know.

Jupiter is another; Mercury, another; Neptune; another, Saturn, another; but there is nothing forcing the Creator to make the same creation on Saturn or Jupiter or Neptune or Venus. No, as He likes, and no one can force Him to show them what is on them.

Allah—you must believe in His greatness and His countless Power Oceans. And His unlimited Will, unlimited Ability, Capability and countless powers of creation are operating. You are so small!

O mankind, come to your real position so that you can see something. If you get so big, expanding beyond your true size, one day you are going to be nothing, disappearing.

May Allah forgive us and grant us a clear understanding to understand something and to be honoured by the Lord of honours. For the sake of the most honoured servant in His Divine Presence, Sayyidina Muhammad—*Fateha!*

What we are speaking about, it is not something that we are taking from this book or from that book, but it is directly coming from Their spirituality, through my Grandshaykh,

---

[13] In every place, there are inhabitants.

to address to you, as well as to all people from East to West, from North to South. ▲

2

THE EMPTINESS OF MATERIAL SATISFACTIONS

A'udhu bil-Lahi min ash-Shaytani-r-rajeem. Bismillahi-r-Rahmani-r-Raheem. La hawla wa la quwwata illa bil-Lahi-l-'Aliyi-l-'Azheem.

Who is the happiest one? The happiest one is the one who is running to find Allah—the best *mashghala*, work.

So many works are occupying people. *Subhana man a'ata kulli qalbin ma yushghaluhu.*[14] The Lord of Heavens, our Creator, just gives to everyone's heart a different desire or different goal, and that person wants to reach that goal or to reach that desire.

There may be now five or six billion people living on earth. You cannot find two persons whose hearts are occupied by the same desire or the same goal that they want to reach. And what is settled in each one's heart either belongs to material aspects or to spiritual aspects. Either a person is going to be occupied by materiality or by spirituality, and people now are just called by countless advertisements for the material aspects of life.

---

[14] Glory be to Him who gave to every heart what occupies it.

Men are living for material aspects. Their dreams are about material aspects when they sleep. When they awaken, they are, in their imagination, imagining material aspects, but material aspects, *Subhanallahi-l-'Aliyyi-l-'Azheem*,[15] can give a person very little contentment or very, very, very little pleasure. And as long as material aspects increase and become more and more, instead of giving their owner pleasure, there is going to be sadness and hopelessness on its owner, making a heavy burden on him, like a person reaching a heap of gold where he is free to take from it as much as he likes.

He may take from it, putting gold in his pockets but not feeling satisfied, and wanting to take more and more and more, filling every pocket; and then when he wants to stand up, he can't because gold is the heaviest metal, and he is in a difficult position with himself. He wants to carry all of it but he can't. And he is never happy to leave it—unhappy with carrying it, unhappy with leaving it.

That is the material aspect that all *ahli dunya*[16] people who are living in our days, the twenty-first century's people, are asking for. All of them want to take more, more, more, but finally they are unable to carry it; so that material aspects do not give pleasure to people.

You heard about that person who had been given not millions but trillions of yens, the first manager of a Japanese car company? He threw himself off a high building and died. That is the example for all people. He had not mil-

---

[15] Arabic: *Subhanallahi-l-'Aliyyi-l-'Azhim*, Glory be to Allah, the Most High, the Almighty.

[16] Arabic: *ahli dunya*, worldly people.

lions but trillions of yens, billions of dollars, billions of pounds, but he was not happy and in pleasure, and he threw himself down from up and died. A big lesson for people!

But everyone wants to do business. For what? To save money—money, money, money, money! And finally, what is going to happen? Even if he has more and more billions, that person is unhappy and that materiality does not give pleasure to him.

Now we are seeing that people do not understand: Allah Almighty, in His kindness, in His compassion and mercy, may give everyone billions, but He knows that His servants are never going to be in pleasure when it is in unlimited amounts. Therefore, He gives, according to His wisdoms, a little bit, a little bit, a little bit. But man is running to reach more, more, more, and saying, "It is no good!"

"O My servant, if a person eats something and he does not know how to put a balance for his eating, he may die. *Sharh*[17]—that is a bad characteristic, perhaps the worst characteristic among mankind." What is that *sharh*? It is not to put a limit on material desires. The same characteristic, it is for all egos, for all mankind. If you do not put a limit, it may kill you—kill you spiritually and kill you, also, materially, from both sides.

Therefore, now, we may look at people, mankind, living on this planet. They are asking for pleasure in their lives, and mostly now people are looking and seeing that pleasure is through riches. They think that if they get richer, there is

---

[17] Arabic: *Sharh*, gluttony, greed, voraciousness. avariciousness.

going to be more pleasure for them, and that is wrong. It is *bil-'aqs*, the opposite of what they are thinking.

But, *Subhanallahi-l-'Aliyyi-l-'Azheem*, glory be to Allah Almighty! Everyone has lost thinking, not thinking about Reality, because material things can't be carried indefinitely. Finished; they can be carried only up to a limit. But they are trying to make a hundred a thousand, and a thousand ten thousand, and ten thousand a hundred thousand, and a hundred thousand a million, and a million a billion, and wanting a billion to be trillions. Everyone wants to make it more, not thinking.

They are all square-headed, all people who are not interested in spiritual aspects. They aren't able to break down that wall and take themselves out of that prison, no. No matter how much you may talk, it has no effect on them, and that is a terrible situation for all mankind. And they reached the top point of their material pleasure on New Year's night. Before New Year's night, they blew up a balloon, wanting to make it bigger, bigger, bigger, bigger, as much as their *nafas*, breath, could blow, and that night they put a needle in it. *Woo-ooo!* At nighttime, it was a big balloon. By morning, it was finished.

No pleasure. They are in a dark and sad area. They are saying, "Ohh-h! Where did my balloon go, leaving me? I tried for one year to make it bigger, bigger, and now in one moment, it has disappeared."

This is an example of all material pleasures for mankind. And another group of people—they are like a handful of people, as Sayyidina Nuh[18] ﷺ, throughout hundreds of years, found only about seventy to eighty people who were asking for real pleasure, asking for their Lord's divine pleasure. All the world's people were not asking. They insisted in front of Sayyina Nuh, saying, "We do not believe in you and your pleasures and what you are promising us. No. Our interest is only material aspects, material desires."[19]

He found only eighty people to put in that Ark. And in every time, people did not welcome their prophets. No prophet was welcomed, from beginning to end—they were not welcomed; rather they assaulted, attacked and fought them, those foolish people who were slaves to their egos.

Their desire is to reach an ocean. Their egos are like a thirsty one, thirsty for physical and material desires. They are running to the ocean to take away their thirst but no matter how much they drink, they get more thirsty. When a thirsty person drinks water, plain water, one cup is enough to take his thirst away. But an ocean can't take it away.

Therefore, those who are interested in material aspects, they are on the wrong way, never getting to be satisfied. They are passing away while they are in the flames of thirst, burning. If you put a cup to their mouths, it never takes away thirst from those people. May Allah forgive us! And those who were calling people to plain water, fresh water, sweet water, prophets, were not welcomed by such peo-

---

[18]Arabic: Nuh, the prophet Noah.
[19]See Holy Qur'an, 7:60, 11:27-35, 21:77, 22/;42, 23:23-26, 25:37, 26:105-118, 29:14-15, 56:9, 71:6-24.

ple—never by common people, but only by a small handful of people.

We are seeing now so many anti-Christ people,[20] who are the representatives of Shaytan. One of them may stand up and address people, and millions of people may follow him. If even one prophet came to speak, they would hit him with stones and with dirty things, and swear at him and want to throw him out or to kill him. "Why," they would say, "why are you preventing us from fulfilling our physical desires? Who are you? We are happy with our physical desires. Why are you coming and preventing us?"

From that time, from the beginning up to today, it has been the same situation. Therefore, now, the whole world is working on one thing: to be more and more and more pleased with their physical and material aspects, but they are *never* going to be pleased by their material possessions or material aspects. But those who are asking for pleasure in their hearts, they understand that they will find it only in the Divine Presence, and the way to the Divine Presence passes through prophets, who are on the way to Allah. Therefore, at every time, we are seeing and finding people either walking or running to find Allah, or asking for *dunya*, which is rubbish and is going to finish.

---

[20]Those who, like the Dajjal, the False Messiah prophesied by the Prophet ﷺ for the End-Time, are calling people to a false paradise, and make wrong seem right and right seem wrong.

May Allah forgive us and bless us to be only for Him and for His holy ways, to follow His precious servants, our guides, prophets, particularly the most honoured and most beloved, most respected servant in His Divine Presence, Sayyidina Muhammad ﷺ.

That is the reason why many westerner are refusing to accept Islam and its prophet—because they want to experience New Year pleasures, and Christmas, also. But we are saying that it is prohibited; all of them are cheating you. But they are running to it. "You must do this. Our happiness is through this."

And I am asking, "What about the next day? Your balloon just—*ooh!*—finished. What are you doing now? Repeat it once again."

They are saying, "We can't do that."

May Allah keep us on His right path! ▲

3

CONCERNING EGO CONTROL

A'udhu bil-Lahi min ash-Shaytani-r-rajeem. Bismillahi-r-Rahmani-r-Raheem. La hawla wa la quwwata illa bil-Lahi-l-'Aliyi-l-'Azheem.

We are in need, daily, of control on ourselves. Have you seen any driver leaving his steering wheel and looking at others? Everyone is careful about his own car, everyone's concern is only his car's control. If anyone's car gets out of control, that means that there should be an accident, harming the driver and destroying his car.

And we, also, each one, if we do not take care to keep control of ourselves, we should be harmed physically, or physically and spiritually (when it is physically, spiritually comes together with it). Therefore, the most important duty, most important responsibility, is for everyone to take care, full care, of controlling himself.

The Prophet ﷺ was speaking to his nation, from his time up to the end. And he was addressing everyone up to the end of the world, to keep his nation in safety and not to be touched by anything that makes them suffer.

If a person causes an accident and breaks his bones, legs, hands, chest, head, he suffers. People take him to the hospital, and the treatment is not an enjoyable thing. No one enjoys himself in the hospital. Have you ever seen someone in a hospital enjoying himself and happy? No. As long as he is in the hospital, he is suffering. When he is taken out, he is joyful, saying, "Oh, I am happy that that treatment finished and now I am done."

He may say, "I suffered for days or months in the hospital. Now I am free. I am okay now, I am getting out." And a person who does not keep himself from causing an accident, he should suffer. Therefore, the Prophet ﷺ was saying, "O people! Everyone keeps his line straight and everyone controls his vehicle. If not controlling, he should suffer"—finished!

The Seal of the Prophets, the most honoured one in the Divine Presence, Sayyidina Muhammad ﷺ, was speaking, addressing people. Only unjust people, only no-mind people, only square-headed people, only *safih*,[21] the lowest level people, only no-mind people, only dishonoured people, only Shaytan's followers are coming in the face of that most honoured one and saying. "You are not a real prophet." And we have a saying in Islam: *"Kamala-l-insan tahta kalamihi."*[22] If you want to know someone's value, make him speak because when he speaks you can quickly understand his level.

---

[21]Foolish, brainless.

[22]A person's perfection/maturity is according to his speech.

Bring a person from a flea market and put him on TV. [Chuckles.] You may say, "Speak a little bit. These people want to hear something from you." And he is going to speak.

What is he is going to say? [Parodies:] "We have, every Sunday, a flea market in Southall, and we have, also, every Thursday a flea market in Dalston."

"Speak!"

"Yes. We also have, on the weekend, a jumble sale in a churchyard, every week. O people, you must look there because it is better for you. You also go and buy something, and bring it to the flea market and we will sell it. Jumble sale is so, so sweet! Each day we are looking in newspapers, and you must also look each day in newspapers, particularly *The Times*, to see where there will be a jumble sale in London." That is his speaking.

Eh, another one; bring someone else. "Speak to people!"

"I may speak."

"What do you do?"

"I sell cats, small dogs, in the animal garden."

"What?"

"Listen to me! If you want a jumping cat, you must see that its hair is short. If you want to use it as a cushion, you must choose one whose hair is long because they always like to sleep in beds. You may put your head—oh-h! It may sing to you, '*Purr-purr, purr-purr, purr-purr, purr-purr*'—so beautiful!"

You can understand what is his level. And if you listen to someone whose speech gives your heart, satisfaction, taking away from your heart, from your mind, darkness and cleaning your intellect, you can understand that his level is high. Yes.

Men's intellect, men's minds, will never be able to reach the level of understanding of the Seal of the Prophets ﷺ.[23] For twenty-three years, he was like a mercy rain, raining on all people who were like a dry field, becoming green with those mercy rains. But those who were like rocks never received anything. What comes on rocks goes down, what comes on the earth grows upward.

Up to today, the non-Muslim world has not taken any care to look and see his ultra-perfection, and to look at his dominion on earth and in the Heavens, and among prophets, among angels. Why? One word of his is enough for them to understand, but they are jealous people.

He was saying one word, the Seal of the Prophets ﷺ: "O people, *nafsuka matiyatuka*."[24] Your physical being represents your ego, the representative of ego is your physical being. That takes us to our interest in eating and drinking and dressing and every kind of physical desire that can be fulfilled. That belongs to our ego, and our ego wants us to fulfill its desires.

---

[23]Muhammad, peace be upon him.

[24]"Your *nafs* [ego [lower self] is your mount." meaning a riding animal that you master and ride on with firm control of its direction.

The Prophet ﷺ was saying, *"Nafsuka matiyatuka."* Your ego is like a horse, like a donkey, like a camel that you can ride on. Your mount was not given to you to leave it like a cow in a meadow, only letting it eat and drink there; it was not given to you for that. It was given to you to ride on it and move. If you have a horse, why not use it? You must use it because it was granted to you for some purpose.

The Prophet ﷺ used a word here that is suitable up to eternity. He did not say, *"Nafsuka dabbatuka,"*[25] not saying that your ego is your animal, your horse or your camel or your donkey, no. What is *matiyah?* Anything that you can ride on and use. In his time, there were no cars, no trains, no planes. There were only donkeys, horses, camels, but his advice is up to eternity. If the life of man on earth were to continue up to the end, his words would keep their value.

"Nafsuka matiyatuka." Your ego is your mount, something that carries you, something that can be used to help people reach their goals, their destinations; and the destinations of people are going to end either in Paradise or in Hells. And that is granted to you. If you use it according your intention, if you control it and ask to send it to your destination, the good, final, last station for you should be Paradise. If you control your mount, that is your *mukafat,*[26] reward—rewarded by reaching Paradise.

If not controlling and leaving your mount, camel or horse or donkey, free to go as it likes, you will never get from Mecca to Medina, or from Medina to Damascus, or from Damascus to Aleppo, or from Aleppo to Istanbul.

---

[25] "Your ego is your mount."

[26] Recompense, reward.

Now you have a car to reach from one point to another. If you do not keep control of yourself, there must be an accident harming you and destroying your car completely. Therefore, Allah Almighty is ordering His servants, "Beware of your egos!" Don't let your ego do as it likes but take control of it so that it is going to be like a Buraq[27] for you, the holy horse coming from Paradise and taking people from here to their Paradise. "

Now people, the twenty-first century's people, they are saying, "We have reached the height of civilization." They are such foolish ones, such no-mind people, such square-headed people, and no one is controlling himself. Because of their egos, no one is taking any care, no. All people are running after their egos, to see how they can make a more enjoyable life for their egos.

They did it a week ago, enjoyment for their egos, the whole world giving trillions and quadrillions of dollars. Did they reach their final goals? No! Now they are longing again for that night. I am saying, "Repeat it!"

And they are saying, "We can't do that. We can only reach it from one year to the next, only for a few minutes in the darkness, and running into the new year. That is our final goal. We reach it once each year, and it is only for minutes, no more."

For what are you doing that? What is the meaning of your egoistical desires' highest limit, highest goal? What is

---

[27] The name of the steed from Paradise upon which the Prophet ﷺ rode during his Night Journey ('Isra).

after that? To where do you want to move? And each year their enjoyments are also coming down, not going up, beginning to come down, to come down.

Perhaps old people are not able to come out of their homes, to go to big squares and dance and shout; only young ones are coming there. Then the old ones are covering themselves up, sitting under roofs, in buildings, and they are saying, "We can't do as they are doing. We can't do it." But they are drinking something that brings imagination to people.

[Chuckles.] Even an old cat, it thinks that it is becoming a tiger. [Laughter.] Oh-oh, one drink! [Parodies:] "O my darr-ling, we may go out!"

"O my darling, if anyone touches me I will fall. Leave that!"

"No-o-o! We are drinking, drinking Irish whisky. Now I am like tiger! Get up!"

Once Grandshaykh[28] was saying to me that a small mouse was inspecting the cellar[29] to see if there was any cheese. And it jumped to reach the cheese, then fell into an open barrel of old wine, and drinking, drinking, drinking. It wanted to get out and it was swimming. Getting out, and it was shouting, "Where are those cats? [Much laughter.]

---

[28]Shaykh 'Abdullah ad-Daghestani, Shaykh Nazim's shaykh, who passed away in 1973.

[29]Here the Shaykh adds parenthetically: "Europeans have cellars because they like to be like tigers, keeping wine to be old and changing its position every time. 'Now it is forty years old. Must come in front and another will go to that side.'"

Where are the cats? Cats can come to me now!" because it had become a tiger. [Shaykh laughs heartily.]

And old people who drink old wine, even if they are ninety years old, they think that—*arrrgh!*—they are now like tigers. "Oh my darr-ling, get up! We may do a dance." [Much laughter.]

"I can't do it."

"Stand up!" [Laughter.]

That is the *tamthil*, metaphor, of peoples' lives in the twenty first century—drunk people, too drunk to see Reality and to reach Reality. Therefore they are rejecting everything that belongs to Heavens and they are going into sewers because they have no control on their egos. And their egos are making them be like comedians, people laughing at them. Finished!

Therefore, if anyone wants to reach heavenly stations, he must be able to control himself to reach his high position, station, in Heavens. If they leave themselves without control, they will never reach even one foot up. They will fall on earth, never going up.

Therefore, all the prophets were coming and saying, "O people, try to make a control on yourselves. If you do not do that, you can't reach your goals. Use your mount in the right way, and you should be happy and should reach eternity." Eternity—so sweet a word! If not, no eternity for you. You are going to be finished and vanish.

And therefore the Prophet ﷺ was saying, "Day by day, this world is approaching its last station. Good ones from among *sultans*,[30] from among learned people, from religious people, from holy ones, day by day they are leaving this life and there are no inheritors for them. Then there should remain on earth only rubbish ones, rubbish ones."

And the Prophet ﷺ was saying as a *tamthil*, example, that a farmer, when the wheat is ready, does like this with this shovel, and the inferior grains go to one side and the good grains go to the other side. Then the farmer puts the good grain in bags and takes it to the warehouse for himself. And the rest, with a broom, *supürüge,* he brushes away because it has no value.

In this world, when the Last Days approach, you are not going to find a good one in power or walking among people. All should be like that valueless grain and straw, to be taken away.

I am asking forgiveness from Allah Almighty and asking not to be from among those people. We are trying to be from among His good servants. O our Lord, keep us from being among the rubbish ones and being thrown away in dustbins. For the honour of the most honoured prophet in His Divine Presence, Sayyidina Muhammad ﷺ —*Fateha!* ▲

---

[30] Rulers, kings.

4

CONCERNING HARMFUL FREEDOM

By the name of Allah, All-Mighty, All-Merciful, Most Beneficent and Most Munificent.

A'udhu bil-Lahi min ash-Shaytani-r-rajeem. Bismillahi-r-Rahmani-r-Raheem. La hawla wa la quwatta illa bil-Lahi-l-'Aliyyi-l-'Azheem.[31] By the name of Allah, Almighty, All-Merciful, Most Beneficent, and Most Munificent.

Crying, not raining—crying on mankind, what is coming on them during this year not raining, crying.

A'udhu bil-Lahi min ash-Shaytani-r-rajeem. Bismillahi-r-Rahmani-r-Raheem. La hawla wa la quwwata illa bil-Lahi-l-'Aliyi-l-'Azheem[32]

They are saying, "Today is a new year. Yesterday was an old year. Today is New Year's Day." People are very

---

[31] "I take refuge with Allah from Satan, the rejected. In the name of Allah, the Beneficent, the Merciful. There is no might nor power except with Allah, the Most High, the Almighty."

[32] I seek refuge in Allah from Satan the accursed. In the Name of Allah, the Beneficent, the Merciful. There is no power or might except with Allah, the Most High, the Almighty.

happy to make this earth seem young as its years increase, saying, "Oh-h-h-h! The old is going, a fresh world is coming. Oh, very good! Good tidings! New year, young year! Our planet is going to be younger because its years are increasing and it is becoming new." *Masha'Allah!*[33]

People have lost their minds. Therefore, I am saying, "*Yahu*,[34] it is also good tidings for me that I am increasing to ninety, so that I will become a new one." What a mentality, what a shaytanic teaching, making everything upside-down, showing lighted worlds as dark worlds, and showing darkness to people as light!

If all people had died yesterday and today was the second day of their death, if you asked what happened, someone would say, "Today is the second day. Now, for two days, they have passed away."

"What happened?"

"Whoever was on the planet just fell down and died, passed away. No more mankind on it, finished!"

Before yesterday, they were in this world. Yesterday they passed away and today there is no longer any sign of them, not one among mankind walking on this earth—finished. But people, they think that this life is a never-ending life.

If it is a never-ending life, that means that it is running like a river. If you stand and look at a river, you think that it is same. No; each moment it changes. It is not same water but flowing, new water coming. People think that that river,

---

[33] As Allah wills.
[34] Turkish expression, meaning, "See here!"

the Volga, Danube, Nile or Amazon, is running, but it is not same water. No; it just flowed away. And people are looking and saying, "Today is the same as yesterday."

No! You can't bring a proof that the people going in the streets, from East to West, from North to South, are the same. No. New ones are coming and so many are passing away. But people think it is the same *dunya*, the same world.

No, it is not. Change is written on everything so that you can't find any creature in this world the same as yesterday. Yesterday, people were in another position—with their thoughts, with their actions, with their movements, with their desires. It was just a hundred per cent different from what they are in today.

Thirteen hours ago, this world was another world, and the people in it—their minds, their goals, their desires, their activities, their thoughts—were different. Now thirteen hours have just passed. Now they are saying, "We have passed from the old ship, from the old vessel, into a new vessel."

Yes! Each day is a chest, but what it carries is different. They are thinking so many things. Thirteen or fourteen or twenty hours ago, all their desires finished and were buried and disappeared. Today is another world for them. And each day gives a perfect lesson to any of mankind who can think.

If they do not think, they are like animals because thinking has not been granted to animals. To think, it is a grant from Allah Almighty to mankind. No other creatures think. No, you can't find one.

Do you think that cats sit like this and think? Perhaps thinking, thinking, sitting in front of the table and looking like this, sometimes looking like that, showing its owner that it is sleeping but from time to time opening its eyes. A cat thinks about *that* point [laughter], or it sits in front of the mouse's hole and does like this. "That mouse is looking at me, and I am preparing myself to catch it because it is New Year's and I must celebrate." [Laughter.] Even if you say, *"Psst-psst-psst,"* the cat will never look at you, very carefully *muraqaba*, observing, that hole, and inside the mouse is doing like this. "Heh-heh-heh, heh-heh!"

Eh-h-h! Only a cat sits and observes very carefully, to catch and to have its breakfast for the honour of the new year—yes?—because New Year's night is important for cats, also, and mice. When men are falling down drunk, they are running at them, jumping on them, cats not looking at mice at that time because there are so many leftover things. And last night, so many *tandhifat ma'mur*, municipal cleaning workers, cats, were so busy that they never slept. Why? Because they were waiting to see how they could reach that, people putting so many things in the municipal *sanduq*, dustbin. Cats were jumping, reaching the top. So many dogs were trying to reach, also, but they are not suited to doing like this, falling down.

Cats were jumping into it and looking. "Heh-heh!" *zakum*.[35] "You are our enemies. Eat poison, O dogs!"

"We [dogs] are here, also. Throw away a little bit!"

---

[35]Gobbling.

"No, no! Eat poison!" [Laughter.]

A very happy night it was, but no thinking. Today, as before, going-coming, going-coming. Last night, no one was thinking and their level was beneath the level of animals. Yes.

Today this is a world; yesterday it was another. It was in another, different, state, and today's state is different from it. So many people who were in existence yesterday and up to midnight, are not in existence today. They passed away, through change, coming, coming.

How, under such conditions, can a person reach *tumanina*, tranquility or contentment, within himself? It is impossible, it is impossible! If you are on a vessel and it is full of passengers, and a big wind storm comes and the waves or the storm take some of the people on it, how can they be in tranquility? And this world now is like those people who are on a ship and a storm just comes on them and—*woo-oo-oo!*—taking them away, and no one is able to stop it or to protect himself. How can they be in peace? Even if they are not at the top of the ship, even if they are in their rooms, even in their rooms they do not feel tranquility in their souls. And now the whole world is in a position like a big vessel on the Atlantic and a storm is just coming on it. Everyone is trembling. No tranquility, no contentment.

Once a famous shaykh, perhaps 'Ubaidullah al-Ahrar Hazretleri, *qaddas-Allah sirruhu al-'aliya*,[36] may Allah bless

---

[36]"*Qaddus Allahu sirruhu al-'aliya*, may Allah sanctify his lofty secret," the invocation for Muslim holy men and saints *(awliya)*.

him, or some other one, was on a ship and a storm broke. All the *mureeds*[37] were just occupied with the safety of their lives. Only one person, he was sitting and keeping with himself a *mangal*, a brazier. And his shaykh came and said, "What are you doing? What are you doing?"

"I am guarding my shaykh's fire."

"Look where your brothers are!"

He looked. All of them were sitting on air by their spiritual powers, not sitting on the ship.[38] Only that one was sitting on the deck. And his shaykh said, "What are you doing?"

"O my shaykh, *an-naru fakihat ush-shitta,* fire is the food of winter. I am keeping this fire here so that it does not fall down and burn the entire ship."

Then the shaykh said to the others who were sitting above, "Oh! What are you doing? From whom did you get that order to sit above, not to be on the ship?" And the shaykh looked with his spiritual power, and all of them—*ooh-h!*—just fell into the ocean.

When they had fallen into the ocean, not drowning, also, he said to them, "You are free people, free from the heaviness of your physical being. No need to go above and sit on air. If you fall into the ocean, the ocean will not accept you, either. You can't drown in it. Come and take your good manners from that one who never changed his posi-

---

[37] Disciples or followers of a shaykh or holy man.

[38] That is, so they would not go down with the ship, they were sitting on air.

tion and is sitting on the ship. Take your good manners from him!"

Tumanina, tranquility, in a difficult position, dangerous situation, is only by being with Allah. Those who are with Allah, no trouble for them, no problem for them, no danger for them, no fear for them, no hopelessness for them. And now we are saying that the whole world is in such a condition. Only *ahadu-n-nass*, certain people who are never affected by what happens on earth, are exceptions because people are just occupied by material aspects, and material aspects make them feel unrestful, hopeless and fearful.

Yesterday they reached the top point of their pleasure. Today, they are just falling down from the highest point, falling from maximum to minimum—finished! And all the world's people who were at the top point of their pleasure yesterday, today they are at the point of zero, below zero, except those who are with Allah. Others, they took their tickets from Shaytan's vessel, and the shaytanic "Transatlantic" brought them to a terrible and dangerous whirlpool. Those who are taking the vessel, the Ark of Noah, the Ark of Safety, Allah Almighty's vessel, they are very few...

Therefore, today is so normal for those people, and yesterday was not any different. They are not saying that we lost yesterday's pleasures. No, normal life is running; routine has not changed for them. But those people who come like this, *"Ah-h!"* are falling down. And they are coming, saying, "Happy New Year!"

I am saying, "It is not today. Tomorrow." [Laughter.] "New year for me is tomorrow. Today is for you. Go away!" But they are not happy. For them, Happy New Year finished from midnight. *Allahu Akbar!*[39]

O people, it is a big Ocean of wisdoms They are giving us,[40] that we may be able to control our desires, to put a limit on them. Without limits, what we are doing is harming us physically and spiritually.

A person was discussing about TV and saying to me, "O Shaykh, we want more freedom and we can't find it through Islam. We are finding it through democracy."

I am saying, *"Pocracy!"*[41] a dirty-smelling system that is just locked down now, everywhere. No country has a key for opening and for cleaning that dirtiness that democracy is pouring on countries.[42] I am asking, "What more freedom than this do you want? If you are want that freedom that is like New Year's midnight, it is impossible to continue it, and the second night, tonight, you can't do it. You can't bring it back, you can't repeat it." Yes; I am saying, "Why do you not repeat it tonight, also?"

---

[39] Allah is Most Great.

[40] Here and elsewhere, "They" refers to the departed high saints of the Naqshbandi Tariqah, from whom Shaykh Nazim's inspirations are derived.

[41] A play on the word democracy substituting it with a derogatory Turkish word.

[42] Through permitting unlimited freedom.

They are saying, "O Shaykh, we are finished, physically finished, financially finished. From every direction, we are finished!"

"Last night you were so happy, and you thought that you had reached the peak of pleasure and enjoyment. Why do you not repeat it tonight?"

"It is difficult."

"Anyone preventing you?"

"No. No one is preventing us but we are finished. We can fill our physical being and our minds for such a night once a year. We can't repeat it."

I am saying, "Repeat it every month!"

"No."

"Three months!"

"No."

"Six months!"

"No."

"Nine months!"

"No. Must be twelve months, once."

Yes, no hindrance for them to repeat it. The government is saying, "If you can do it, do. You are free." But no, no one. They are saying, "We are finished."

We understand that democracy, which that foolish one was discussing with me and saying that democracy is the most perfect system for nations, to give people their freedom. And I was saying, "Why not use that freedom every night as you used it on New Year's midnight? Repeat it!" And they are such foolish ones, asking for that freedom every day, every hour. And I am saying, "Who is preventing you now? Repeat it! Make it every night."

Therefore, democracy, the system of complete freedom, may be a fully harmful system, first killing their spirituality, then taking their physical being and also breaking it, as a meat-grinding machine breaks meat with bones and it goes out. But people are still running after democracy. *Yahu*, it is not suitable! You can't carry democracy for even two nights; you are waiting for one year to repeat it. How are you asking for that freedom and its activities to be every day, every hour, to give people *mutlaq*, absolute, freedom to do everything? No!

Therefore I am saying that Islam is the best, Islam is the best. Christianity is has lost its power to affect people, just as Judaism is has lost that power. Islam is the best, keeping people at their normal capacity and normal ability. They may do everything according to its own reality.[43] That is important.

Therefore, Islam says, "You may do this, you can't do that." That is perfection, not to be like the craziness of the democratic system that leaves people free to do everything; no. That is only for cattle in the meadow; *they* can do that, or in the jungle wild animals can do everything as they like. Or as each night on *Discovery* they are showing people under the seas, under the oceans. There you can find everything that they can do. But for man, the best way of life is in

---

[43] In a realistic manner, according to what is good for people and they are capable of.

Islam. Islam gives freedom when we are in need of it and prevents it when it is going to be harmful to you and others.

May Allah forgive us and give us a good understanding of Islam. For the honour of the most honoured one in His Divine Presence—*Fateha!*[44] ▲

---

[44] The opening *surah* [chapter] of the Qur'an.

5

THE CRITICAL NEED FOR A GLOBAL CHANGE

A'udhu bil-Lahi min ash-Shaytani-r-rajeem. Bismillahi-r-Rahmani-r-Raheem. La hawla wa la quwwata illa bil-Lahi-l-'Aliyi-l-'Azheem.

O our Lord, *ya Rabbana*, gather our hearts to hear, from Your divine station—to be gathered and listen and obey. Understand?

When you collect water, much more power comes for turning the mill. If that water is spread over a wide space, it is weak; can't turn. Therefore, the mill always collects the water, when coming on the stones to turn them, not letting it flow in a wide space—no; collecting, collecting, collecting. Then it gives that power.

Therefore, we are asking from Allah Almighty to do everything for His sake, for His glory, for His divine honour. Everything that you are going to do, you must do it for His divine glory and divine pleasure. That is important!

When you want to do something for Him, Almighty, you must gather your every power. Therefore we are saying, *"Allahu Akbar!"*[45] That means we are putting away everything that occupies us and making ready all our spirituality, and also our physical being, to be a hundred per cent present in His Divine Presence. If not, it is so wide a space, [unlike the mill], never turning.

Yes; power. That is important, to collect your whole power. You must think about it: In whose Presence am I standing now? Whom am I addressing now? Whom am I worshipping now? Therefore we are saying, *"Allahu Akbar,"* putting aside everything because nothing is valuable in comparison to what we are doing.

There is deep heedlessness now. People think that their works, their business, their efforts, their doing of everything that belongs to this life is important. I am saying, "Come and give your obedience to your Lord who created you."

They are saying [parodies], "No time. No time for praying because we have so many thing to do."

They do not think that the most important work for man is to stand up and pray for the sake of his Lord's divine glory—to do *that* work, obedience, for His divine glory. Instead, people think that this life and their works are so important, so important, saying, "No. No time."

"What are you doing? Rubbish! What you are doing will finally go to the W.C.[46] For what are you doing this?"

---

[45]The *takbir*, meaning "Allah is Most Great," uttered by Muslims at the beginning and at each change of posture during prayers.
[46](Brit.) toilet.

Satan is showing them that what they are doing is so important. "I am the President, I am the Prime Minister, I am a minister, I am a mayor, I am a governor, I am the King, I am the Queen, I am the *Sultan*, I am the biggest director, manager, of this or that company, or I am the chairman of this bank or that bank," they are thinking. They think that these titles that they give make their works so important, while for obedience they are saying, "No time to look at such things. We are busy!"

What is this? Such a mentality is bringing the whole world to the worst condition, for which they will never find a solution. The whole world's people, all of them, have just fallen into a dark and narrow place, and they are hopeless and full of fear for their future.

The U.S. is saying, "In 2004, we are making big plans and projects, and planning only for war, not anything else. We are preparing every department, everything, only for war in 2004, no other project, because we must pass this narrow strait safely. Then we can think about it. Now we see that we are in the most dangerous situation and in the most terrible conditions."

That is the statement of the U.S., which is the superpower and patron on earth. Due to *that* they are saying this. What about others? All countries are now only thinking about preparing for their defense—how they will be able to protect themselves, small ones and big ones. The small ones are preparing themselves: "We may take the side of the U.S." Others may say, "We can take our way with Russia or China or other big countries. We can be under their wing, and we must also be prepared ourselves."

No country feels safe about its future. Germany, France, England, Russia, China, Pakistan, India, Japan, Arabs, Turks—none of them feels that it is in safety. None of them looks at its future and says to itself, "We have a guarantee through our power," no one. That is the result of the heedlessness of people, because they are throwing away the first important duty that they should keep, to be their Lord's obedient servants. Always they are kicking away that obedience, but yet they are asking for a safe way. They can't find it! Personally or collectively or globally, safety is impossible if they throw away obedience to their Lord, Almighty Allah.

That is biggest crisis for mankind. No one is hopeful and fearless about his future, no. Even the U.S. is finished because people are throwing away the most important thing: to be obedient to their Lord, to keep obedience to the Divine Presence of the Lord of Heavens. The first punishment is coming for that.

They think that through their weapons they will reach something, but with their weapons they should only reach *damar*, destruction, all buildings down and fields full of dead bodies. That is the result because they are trusting in their weapons and the whole world is trusting in its technology.

Their hope and trust is in their technology. They think that when they use high technology, they should be able to reach their goals on earth—a safe life and a peaceful and enjoyable life. They do not think that another technology may come and destroy *their* technology. And the boss of the superpowers, U.S.A., is saying, "In 2004, we are planning and making every project and plan only for war." Therefore, no hope for all the world's people for tomorrow. *"Fa'tabiru."*⁴⁷ Take your lessons, O people, from what Allah Almighty is sending to us, saying, "Only *I* give peace. I am the only One who can give peace to you, to your life. But as long as you are not obedient servants to Me, until you make My obedience, My servanthood, the first aim, you are never going to reach peace or a peaceful, enjoyable life in this world. You can't, you can't reach that!

Therefore, this world must be changed. We are the smallest state on earth, and the Northern Turkish government is coming and asking me, "Do you think that we are in need of a change?"

I am saying, "Yes. You need a change because your condition now is the worst. If you insist on not changing, you are never going to reach a good and hopeful and peaceful life because you are on wrong way. You are kicking away obedience to your Lord and He is punishing you so that you can't reach a peaceful life. You must change yourselves," I am saying to them.

And now I am saying to the whole world that they must change their way if they want a peaceful life, a peaceful world, global peace. If you like that, you must change, you must change your position. Now you are servants of Shaytan. You must change; you must be servants of your Lord, and everything is going to be changed. If not, no one, no technology, can help. Technology has only come for destruction and to take away everything on the face of this

---

⁴⁷*"Then learn a lesson [or, take warning]."* (59:2)

earth, and to remain only ashes and dead bodies and broken buildings and destroyed cities. That will be the result.

This is a warning from Spiritual Headquarters[48] to all nations. If they listen and change, they should reach a safe and peaceful life. If not, they know! They can do as they like, but they are never going to be welcomed with a good life, a peaceful life. Always they should be faced with troubles, crises, wars, fighting, destruction, sufferings and miseries here, before the Day of Resurrection.

May Allah forgive us and send us some ones from His saints, from His valued servants, honoured servants, to turn our faces from the wrong direction to the right direction, to leave Shaytan and to be with Allah. For the honour of the most honoured one in His Divine Presence, Sayyidina Muhammad —*Fateha!* ▲

---

[48] All living saints live under an established hierarchy of command, through which they receive their orders and inspirations. The "spiritual headquarters" refers toShaykh Nazim's master, Grandshaykh 'Abdullah ad-Daghestani who receives directly from the Prophet.

6

CHOOSING ACCEPTABLE, RIGHT ACTIONS

A'udhu bil-Lahi min ash-Shaytani-r-rajeem. Bismillahi-r-Rahmani-r-Raheem. La hawla wa la quwwata illa bil-Lahi-l-'Aliyi-l-'Azheem. It is an Association,[49] to wake up people.

If Allah Almighty had not sent His prophets, peace be upon them, to mankind, and especially the last, the Seal of the Prophets, the Honour of Creation, the most honoured servant in the Divine Presence, for whose honour all creatures were created, [we would not have any criteria for our actions]. All the prophets, they were sent to mankind to show them what is wrong and what is right; because man has been granted a will, granted a mind, and granted a physical being so that, acting within his area of permissibility, he has been granted to do something.

A man is not a solid figure, motionless, not doing anything. Rather, we have been created to act, and our physical system in its foundation and the manner of its creation is prepared to move and act.

---

[49] Arabic, *suhbah;* Turkish, *sohbet,* meaning to associate or keep company with the shaykh.

Allah Almighty is the Designer and Creator of mankind. No one can design or think of such a figure as ours. Our outward aspects and the inside are so perfect in their design, and in our faculties or in the specialized actions that we do.

He is able to design our outward aspects and make the inside solid. But He does not do that. The inside is not closed, a solid piece of flesh, no. If you think about it, it makes you more astonished that you have such things inside you that you don't know about—so many organs inside ourselves, and we do not even know what is inside.

So many systems in our physical being! So many veins, and they say that there are veins as fine as a hair or finer, and running through those veins there is blood. And He does not make cells sealed in their *kibaru*, size. Such small cells, one next to the other; each one keeps its position and each one also keeps the rights of the ones next to it. And those thinner-than-hair veins are reaching and pouring into each cell what it needs, according to its nature. What we eat, drink, breathe, veins take that and reach, coming and knocking at each cell.

Each cell has a special entrance, not coming to it from everywhere. That is the order of the Creator: *"Wa atu-l-buyuta min abwabiha."*[50] Each cell is like a special place, a special home, and Allah is ordering, "If you want to enter your homes, you must use their doors." Therefore, each cell has a special entrance, so that even the thinnest veins must *yastadhin*, ask permission. "Is it ready for me to bring something?" And it is answers, "Yes. Bring it." And the veins

---

[50]*"And enter houses by their doors."* (2:189)

are saying, "We are bringing full ones," and the cell is saying, "Take the empty, used ones. Bring new," and taking away, like natural gas tanks, the *yust'amal*, used-up, ones.

In such a way, for those billions and billions of cells, this process goes on with each breath. This breath that we take from the air goes in, going through blood carried by the thinnest veins, reaching every cell, giving fresh oxygen, and taking away each one's used CO_2, carbon dioxide.

It is impossible to think *how* it goes on. That is the greatness that the Lord of Heavens, designing and creating. The circulatory system or digestive system or *'asabi*, nervous system, all work in the utmost perfection. And at the same time, you can see, you can hear, you can talk; at the same time, you can grasp, you can walk, you can feel, you can think, and you can eat, you can drink, and you can sleep, also. When sleeping, no longer is your will working on it.

"*Huwa-l-ladhi yusawwirukum fil-arham.*"[51] He is the only One who designs you and creates you in the darkness of the wombs of your mothers. Those foolish doctors, they want to involve themselves, to put their wills there. They say, "We are controlling it."

Who are you to control? What is this foolishness? Such ignorance with them! How can you claim this? Your control is to put a measuring tape on a woman's waist and say, "Oh, now it is bigger. In one month, it is going to be one centimeter, two centimeters bigger. Okay?" Then putting her on the scale: "Yes, now you are growing, going to be ten stone."[52] And they are putting this and listening to the heart

---

[51] "*It is He who forms you in the wombs [as He wills].*" (3:6)

[52] A stone is British measure of weight, equivalent to fourteen pounds.

of the new creation in the womb of its mother. That is their control. And they are saying to women, "You must come. We must control you." Who are *you* to control? Each time they are involving themselves, it gets worse, the new creation.

When you are thirsty, your body is going to fall down. *Subhanallah*, you may drink one cup of water and then quickly stand up. How did it reach everywhere? How can it be?

The Creator created and designed man as such a miraculous being, *subhanallahu-l-'Aliyu-l 'Azheem!* If for years, a hundred years, even a thousand years, you could think about it, you couldn't find an end to knowledge about the creation of man and his workings. *Subhanallah!* No one can think of such a design, such handsome and beautiful designs!

We are coming to this point, that we have been created in such a manner and design, and we are a working figure of flesh. That figure, thousands of books aren't able to give a description of it. And we do *something*; everyone does *something*. And that something that we have been asked to do, to work on, is because we are not, as we said, solid figures, not moving. No, we are moving.

Those movements are ordinary movements. But the Lord of Heavens, our Creator, is giving His statement to such a perfectly-designed creature through His chosen servants, prophets, saying to all mankind, "O mankind, we have been sent on behalf of your Creator, because it is not according to His divine wisdoms to address everyone directly. He is only addressing and choosing one among yourselves, and through that one He is addressing you."

Therefore, prophets' words are Allah Almighty's words. You must accept this. *"In huwa illa wahyun yuha[53]— it is nothing but what is revealed,"* coming from the Lord of Heavens, and when you hear it, you must hear that Allah is addressing you.

"We have been sent to you, O mankind, to teach you or to show you what you are doing—among your actions, which ones are acceptable and which are unacceptable in His Divine Presence. We have come to show you wrong movements, wrong actions, and right actions, correct actions."

And they brought the balance. From time to time, prophets brought the heavenly balance to mankind according to man's level of understanding. And the last balance, He, Almighty, sent through His most honoured and glorified servant in His Divine Presence with His divine Message to all mankind, to teach and to show them which are right movements and actions, and which are wrong.

That must be taught to the children of mankind, nothing else. If you are able to learn this heavenly teaching that was sent from Heavens, then you may build your life on a very strong foundation, never going to fall or to be destroyed by Shaytan and his followers and supporters and workers. They can't destroy that foundation.

But it is a sad thing that people in the twenty-first century, 2004, are not asking and no one is taking care about

---

[53]*"It is not but a revelation revealed."* (53:4)

such true teachings that make people establish their lives on a powerful foundation and be protected here and Hereafter, and reach eternal peace, eternal enjoyment, eternal happiness, eternal life. Therefore, they have just fallen into a bottomless crisis. They are shouting, some of them are stepping on others, and this world that we are seeing now, it is so bad, so dark, so violent that you can't imagine.

This is the result of people's not using the heavenly balance that shows them whether their actions are good or bad, whether they are right or wrong. They are not using that balance; they have just thrown it away and this is a punishment for them. And till they change and ask, their situation will go from bad to worse, from worse to worst. No way for their safety; no one can save them from this most dangerous situation. Only by a hand from Heavens, if they grasp it and hold it, can they be protected, and others are going to be thrown away like rubbish thrown into a dustbin.

May Allah give us good understanding to follow the heavenly declaration, the heavenly program, what is programed for mankind, because people have changed it and they are falling down into Hells. When we come and follow the heavenly program on earth, we should reach happiness and eternal life throughout eternity.

For the honour of the most honoured one in His Divine Presence, Sayyidina Muhammad ﷺ—*Fateha!* ▲

7

TODAY'S "TOP POINT OF CIVILIZATION"

A'udhu bil-Lahi min ash-Shaytani-r-rajeem. Bismillahi-r-Rahmani-r-Raheem. La hawla wa la quwwata illa bil-Lahi-l-'Aliyi-l-'Azheem. By the Name of Allah, the Lord of Heavens, our Creator.

We are asking forgiveness for our wrong actions, wrong doings, wrong intentions, wrong beliefs, wrong works; we are asking forgiveness. And if He, Almighty, forgives His servant, that means taking him from the wrong way and putting him on the right way. Then you must be thankful to Allah Almighty, and for being thankful, the first thing is to say, "Thanks be to my Lord who saved me from the wrong way and guided me, putting me on His right way."

What is the wrong way and what is the right way? All prophets came and brought the same declaration from Heavens. And through their holy books[54] that include the

---

[54]That is, the divinely-revealed scripture granted to Abraham, no longer in existence; the original Torah/ *Taurat* to Moses; the *Zabur*, possibly in-

heavenly declaration, they made clear to mankind about their lives, about themselves on this planet, *Dunya*, the world. And then they also made clear to us that there is another life that you can't reach till you pass from this life to that life. That means that death takes you from this life to another life that is veiled. You can't see it till you die. If you have not died, those veils can't be opened to you, but when you die they are opening.

Therefore, prophets came and said that you must believe that after this life, which is a temporary one, you will reach a permanent life. That is a belief that has never changed from first one, the first prophet, to the last one—I mean to say, from Adam ﷺ to the Seal of Prophets after Jesus Christ, the most honoured prophet and the last messenger from the Heavens to the earth, Sayyidina Muhammad ﷺ. This, first of all, is the right path for all nations, for all mankind.

When Allah Almighty forgives His servant, he is going to know about this temporary life and, after it, about the permanent life or eternal life. The wrong way for people is not to think about it. Ninety-nine percent or more of people now do not think about it. They think that life is granted to them only once and that it is, also—according to their imagination, according to their thinking, according to their claims—by accident, *tasaduf*, coincidence.

They are saying that our life happens with no balance or measure. No one makes a *dilekçe*, application, to come this life. Does anyone write a application and ask, "May I come and be on earth"? No. It is a grant to us, but people

---

cluding some of the Psalms, to David; the *Injil*, the original Gospel, to Jesus; and the Holy Qur'an to Muhammad, peace be upon them all.

now are saying that it is an accident or coincidence. "It is a chance that we came, that we are in this life." And what is beyond this life no one thinks about, particularly in our time when all religions and their beliefs have gone down.

People who lived thousands of years ago were with their prophets. But no nation welcomed its prophets. The Lord of Heavens sent His representatives, His messengers, to speak to people about unchangeable realities, but nations did not welcome them, and they wanted to attack them, to fight them, and, if they were able, to kill them.

That is the characteristic of no-mind people who are donkeys for their egos—donkeys, because they are running to the meadows and fighting their riders. Their riders want to take them to the King's feast but their donkeys are saying, "No, we don't want to go there. We are enjoying grass in the meadows."

And now, people are in such a way. They are saying, "It is enough for us to enjoy ourselves in the meadows. For what shall we go? You say that there is the King's feast but we do not see it," and they are denying it.

Now all nations are denying, including Turks and Arabs, also. Pakistanis and all the Muslim world, they are not keeping real faith. They are also looking to the life that they are in now and they are not interested in eternal life, the life after death—no. They are saying, "Our job is to be here, to arrange our life as our egos like, to make our egos happy and joyful during this life, and no more. We are running after this goal only. After death, as you say, there is a permanent life. We are not interested in it."

Those wrong ideas are just carrying people into this crisis that now the whole world has fallen into and they do not know how they can save themselves from it. The Seal of the Prophets ﷺ, as well as other prophets, was informing people that when the Last Days approach, nations are going to fight among themselves internally. Let alone neighbours, they are trying to fight among themselves.

"Every country, O Shaykh? For example, now America is the patron of the world and its power is reaching from East to West, from West to East, and it is fighting another country. How you are saying that all nations will fight internally?"'

Yes, because of the *iqtidar*, the power that they are holding in their hands. In every country there is a government that holds power for governing the country. Each group wants to reach power, yes. When reaching power and beginning to do something as they like, in front of them there are some other groups that are unhappy. They are saying, "You are wrong, doing wrong things. Go away! *We* must come."

Mukhalafah, opposition—prediction of that is a miracle of the Seal of the Prophets. At the beginning, they claimed that there is no opposition in democracy. All of them were against the nobility—kings and queens or emperors or *sultans* or *shahs*. But after that, Shaytan was still unhappy so he put in front of the common people in 1789 a big revolution, the French Revolution. That was the worst revolution. Other, even worse revolutions followed that.

That was the beginning. They killed all the nobility in France who were in power and they put *their* people instead—not as they were advertising, no. And those people opened the doors of the Bastille [to lawless elements], saying, "Come and do as you like now. You can establish your state, your governing body. You can do it." You can do to the nobility as violent animals in the jungle do. Little ones and adults, men and women, they took them away, killing them under the guillotine.

They were in opposition to the King, monarchy. They finished it. Then Shaytan was saying, "I don't want mankind to be in peace. Come now!" Saying to this one, "Why are you letting that one be at the point of power? You are much more suitable for that. Why are you going to be under his command? No! You must oppose them, you must establish an opposition group. Ha-ha!"

Then they made these two parties, the one-party system finished. "Now you must keep democracy. Everyone may form a party and everyone must try to reach power." That is the meaning of the Prophet's saying that every nation is going to fight within itself, not outside.

America is fighting now, opposing the President and his party. In Turkey, oppositions are fighting the government that is in power. In Russia, the same; in Greece the same. In our small state, Turkish Cyprus, also, opposition groups are fighting each other, and we are only a handful of people. In Egypt, internal fighting; in Libya, in Saudi Arabia, in Pakistan. In England, people are saying, "You are wrong, Tony Blair, you are doing wrong. We are coming to do it in the right way to reach power."

Yes; they are fighting. Do you not see on TV how they are fighting each other? That is the miracle of the Seal of

Prophets ﷺ, that he was saying fifteen centuries ago what is going to happen when the Last Days approach.

O people, use your minds! O people, think about it! O people, follow the Prophet's advice! Otherwise, Shaytan is going destroy everything on earth, and out of six billion, five billion are going to die! There may be left only one billion on earth, and Shaytan will be so happy.

But people are drunk now. How are they saying now that we are happy here? No one is happy. Only those people who are living for their Lord, they are happy, their faces lighted, their hearts in satisfaction, their lives in peace, and no fear of coming days, here or Hereafter. And they are a handful of people.

All other people, all other people should be punished. Shaytan never sits. Shahu Naqshband,[55] the main pillar of the Most Distinguished Naqshbandi Order, was saying, "I was looking to find Shaytan taking a rest, even for one moment. But at every moment he is busy. For what? To make people fall into crises, troubles, problems, and to be always in suffering. I never caught him resting even a little bit. No, working hard!"

And now Shaytan is saying, "I am reaching the last point of my effort, *sa'i*—finished! I am going to destroy everything on earth because I wanted to be the deputy on earth, and the Creator, for the sake of Adam and his children, did

---

[55]Shah Bahuddin Naqshband Muhammad al-Uwaisi al-Bukhari, the great fourteenth century Central Asia *wali* who founded the Naqshbandi *Tariqat*.

not give it to me. Now I have reached the point of taking away Adam and his descendants, and I am going to put my power, my dominion, on earth. Just one step now, waiting!"

And people are not thinking about it and they are running after Shaytan. And they are saying, "Our lives are only here. We do not believe in the future. After death, nothing!"

They are playing music, they are running in the streets. "O people, where you are going?"

"We are going to the celebration!"

"Where?"

"In front of a *heykal*, a statue."[56]

"You are not going to the mosque?"

"No need! We do not believe in mosques, we do not believe in churches, we do not believe in synagogues. Our Lord is only the one whose statues we are making, and he is coming and speaking through them."

O people, tomorrow is going to be much heavier for unbelievers. Tomorrow there is going to be more darkness for them because, for everything that they are trying to do, there is no result. Every door is just closed in front of them and they can't find any key to open it. But they are not coming to me to give to them the key.

---

[56] Referring to the statues of Kemal Atatürk, the earlier dictator of Turkey, whose secular ideals and opposition to Islam still dominate Turkish life and thought.

We have the key; we have the key for the whole world. If they come, we may give the key of Islam—Islam, that concerns all mankind, individually and collectively, offering what they may be in need of. When they come and fall into a dangerous situation, we have the key to open it. The Lord of Heavens just sent it for the happiness of mankind.

They are trying every religion now, mankind. "They are making so many laws, *kanun*," they are saying, looking at the Old Testament. "We can't use it." Looking at the New Testament, saying, "Nothing in it. We must leave it; we must look at Buddhism."

"Buddhism, it is not suitable for our lives. Hinduism!"

"Then no one will be able to buy a cow. Can't do it! And everyone will be running after his cow with a pot, to put it into when it does something at the back. It is not suitable for us. [Laughter.] It is enough for us to clean our dogs' dirt."

It is written on an *amud*, a post, in the streets of civilized European municipalities, *belediyeler*, "Dog keepers must carry a box and brush when they go out, and when their dogs make dirt, they must clean it. Otherwise, there is a *jeza'*, penalty." Therefore, [chuckles] dog lovers are carrying around some small dogs, with a small box on their shoulder; a small brush, also. There is also a dog like a small donkey for them, a big one. One here, one there; some people are going out with two dogs, one running like this, another like that, and they are doing here, doing there. That person is confused. "How can we manage two pots?"

Shaytan is making honoured mankind to be dogs' servants, leaving the servanthood of their Lord and trying to be the servant of dogs. *La hawla wa la quwwata . . . !* How is this *dunya*, how is this world, how are these nations going to be successful? What is this system of theirs?

[Facetiously:] Cows are a hundred times better for carrying away their dirt. But Europeans, who claim to be civilized people, the top of civilization for them is to be the servants of dogs. *Ya'ayibu*—a shame for humanity, a big shame!

If I say, "Keep a goat in your home," they are saying, "No, no. We are not farmers."

"Put hens and a cock."

"The *belediye*, municipal council, is prohibiting it because the cock crows. They say, 'We can't sleep because its crowing disturbs us.'"

They are thinking in such a way, all the wrong way. That is the wrong way that we are speaking about now. I am here. If anyone brings any objection to it, I am here to answer it. But it is enough for those who have something in their heads of intellect or mind.

We must change ourselves, O Europeans, who are claiming, "We have reached the top of civilization." The top of civilization for Western people is to sleep with dogs and to carry dogs and to be the servants of dogs; that is the top point of civilization. And the Prophet ﷺ was saying, "Don't keep dogs in your homes." Dogs may only be used for herding, not everywhere; no.[57]

---

[57]That is, as working animals used to herd flocks and guard premises, not for keeping in the house as pets.

May Allah forgive us! It is a long story. Those who are going to wake up may look and accept Reality. They should be saved here and Hereafter. If not, they should be punished here and in eternity.

May Allah forgive us and send us some of His beloved servants to bring nations into the right path, the right way, to be saved here and Hereafter. For the honour of the most honoured one in the Divine Presence, Sayyidina Muhammad ﷺ—*Fateha!* ▲

8

LIVING BREATHS AND POISONED BREATHS

A'udhu bil-Lahi min ash-Shaytani-r-rajeem. Bismillahi-r-Rahmani-r-Raheem. La hawla wa la quwwata illa bil-Lahi-l-'Aliyi-l-'Azheem.

Subhanak! Subhanak! Subhanak![58] Breathing—we are living and breathing, one breath coming, one going; in and out. Your life is just established on two kinds of breaths, and they are informing and teaching us.

Two kinds. One breath is *hayy*, a living breath. The other breath is without life, *ölü*, dead. Living, non-living; living breath, non-living breath. Living breaths are a grant from Allah Almighty to His servants, and non-living breaths are a curse from Heavens,. That is an important point.

And you—you are *mukhayyar*;[59] you have been allowed to choose one of the two, living breaths or non-living breaths. *Tuba*, so much happiness for those people whose breaths are living breaths! Living breaths, they specially

---

[58] Glory be to You (three times).
[59] Having the choice or option.

come from Heavens. And it is a pity, the biggest *hirman*, deprivation, for a person not to reach a living breath.

As our spiritual masters, our grandshaykhs, were saying—my Grandshaykh was saying, also—each one of mankind, during twenty-four hours, has 24,000 breaths. You breathe 24,000 breaths in twenty-four hours. That is a mixture of living breaths and non-living breaths.

How can you reach living breaths? This is a very important point for the lives of mankind. The specialty of living breaths is that they give you new pleasure through your physical being, giving refreshment. If you breathe from those living breaths, they give you new life. And the second kind, non-living breaths, their specialty is to take away from the *sirr 'ata*, the secret grant to you, taking it away.

Who are these and who are those among people? For every action that you are going to do, you need those breaths. When you are going to do an action for your servanthood to Allah Almighty, there reaches you, through that action, living breaths. Therefore, *'abid*, people who work for their servanthood, if you look at them, you find them always fresh, not coming down—fresh, their lifepower never getting less. That living breath gives them more refreshment to stand up. And those people who are running away from Allah, if you say to them, "Come and pray *Jum'ah* prayer,"[60] they say, "We are busy, we have business."

Allah Almighty says, "When the muezzin calls you to the Friday prayer, leave everything and come,"[61] but you do

---

[60] The Friday congregational prayer.
[61] Qur'an, 62:9.

not leave it. Doesn't matter to the caller, muezzin, but it harms you, because, when you work at that time, that non-living breath is poison for you,[62] bringing you down. If you get one million pounds, it can't bring back what you have lost for your structure, for your physical being. And what you have lost spiritually, you can't bring any measure for your loss.

People are saying, "Oh, no time for praying." But prayer-time breaths give you life, making you alive, fresh, nothing touching you, nothing harming you. You are under protection, heavenly protection.

"No. We are busy. We are busy with our business. No time. We are presidents, we are prime ministers, we are M.P.s, we are mayors, we are commanders, we are big business people."

You may be. You may be, but that that title will never give a chance to you to breathe live, alive breaths. What is the benefit?

But people now are mindless. Go to hospitals—full! And every home is also full of ill people—hundreds, thousands, millions. And governments are saying, "We can't reach them."

I heard that in England the government wants to close down hospitals, saying, "We can't reach people. We are giving so many things and *bütçe*, budgeting, from our treasury but we can't reach everyone. We are trying to treat a hun-

---

[62]Meaning that when you continue working instead of fulfilling your obligation to Allah by attending the obligatory weekly congregational prayer, any breath you take is non-living and poisonous.

dred today and we think that they will become less, but tomorrow two hundred will come. Today, one thousand, and we are saying, 'Oh! We sent away one thousand, and two thousand have come in their place.'" And go and look at Turkish hospitals. Here, also. Go and look, because people are breathing poison.

Non-living breaths are making them down and crushing their physical being, poisoning them, because they are running away from their Lord's obedience and servanthood. No chance for them to live a happy life, a peaceful life here—no. It is forbidden for them.

This is a very important point that people must understand. If they understand, this world is going to be changed into paradise—not the after-this-life Paradise, but, according to their condition, this planet is going to be a paradise, no one, no one worrying about their future, no one suffering in their daily lives; sleeping in safety, working in safety. Before asking for it, everything that they want the Lord of Heavens will send. "So My servants will not be tired, so My servants will not be worried, so My servants will not suffer, so My servants will be in the best conditions during this temporary life before coming to Me for the eternal life."

O people, we are speaking, *alhamdulillah*,[63] the truth, the real truth. We are speaking about people's sufferings—the real source of sufferings and miseries and wars and fighting and violence, and no success, no victory, no rest in people's minds or in their bodies, and we are telling the reasons of

---

[63]Praise be to Allah.

hopelessness for people. But I am looking and seeing that people are just forbidden to think.

Yes, there are poison breaths and living breaths. You are free to choose this or that. Therefore, Allah Almighty is saying, *"Inna-l-ladhina amanu wa 'amalu-s-salihati*[64] — to those who believe in Me and keep My servanthood, I am granting to them, here and Hereafter."

People are not listening. They are running after Shaytan. And Shaytan is saying, "Come to me. I shall give you something that no one else can give you. I shall give you refreshment, everything free for your egos." But he is hiding this secret — that the atmosphere, air or breath, that they breathe through that disobedience is poisoning them — poisoning them! And only Satan knows this, but he is hiding it and urging people to come after him, and he is saying, "Do everything as you like!"

And look! This person is not fasting, that person is fasting. This one eats, that one eats.[65] Which one gets more taste? Does a never-fasting person get a good taste or a fasting person? Simple example. No one can reach the happiness or pleasure of the one who is fasting and breaking his fast; even kings, queens or the richest ones can't reach what a fasting person reaches when he opens his fast.

But Shaytan is making his agents, hundreds, thousands, millions of agents, to advertise, "O people, come! Enjoy yourself. Enjoy yourself!" But they are not enjoying. When they go to enjoy themselves, entering into a casino, a pub,

---

[64]*"Indeed, those who believe and do righteous deeds."* (2:277; 10:9; 11:23; 18:30, 107; 19:96; 31:8; 41:8; 85:11; 98:7)

[65]When breaking his fast.

into such people-deceiving places, they are coming out in a worse condition. But Shaytan's advertising is so much!

They are, all of them, poisoned, poisoning themselves with poisoned breaths. Everyone who works for Shaytan is breathing non-living breaths that make our physical being come down, crash; and sorrow, sorrow that you can't imagine, cover their souls.

People must change their ways, their ideas, their directions if they want to reach happiness here and Hereafter. Allah Almighty sent His prophets with such secret realities and secret favors to reach His servants—unknown favors, unknown pleasures. You can imagine a person who is granted pleasure from His Lord. He may be in a terrible prison but his world is Paradise. Someone may be on a throne and on his head a crown, everything made for him or for her, but his feelings are making him be in the worst prison. And people are running to prisons, leaving free palaces, paradises, and running to hells, hells!

Therefore, the Prophet ﷺ was saying, "At the end-time of the world there should come Satan's representative, Dajjal, the Anti-Christ.[66] Before the Anti-Christ, there will come thirty anti-Christs, each one making people to run into Hells and saying, 'This is Paradise,' and keeping people from Paradise and saying, 'This is Hells.'" Yes.

What we said now, it is the truth. Those anti-Christs have just made all the world's people run to hells, to enjoy

---

[66]Dajjal, the False Messiah prophesied in numerous *ahadith* for the end-time of this world.

themselves. They are asking to enjoy themselves, but if they enjoy themselves at nighttime, in the daytime they are finished.

They are going to hospitals and they are suffering from unknown illnesses now. Professors, physicians, are saying, "We never met such a patient before. We do not know any medicine for those people. They are coming every day. We are looking in our books, never finding what their illness is, new kinds of illnesses coming to make people suffer."

Shaytan is making them work at nighttime, calling them, "O people, come to my paradise!" Every dirty place for which they are dressing up belongs to egos. At nighttime, they think that their dressing is so fashionable, using every ornament for themselves, coming in those finest, new-fashion cars. They are running, running to the places of the sources of sufferings, running to be poisoned, and when coming out they are finishing. But no time for people to think about it! They are working like donkeys all day, and at nighttime they think, "We are enjoying." That is the general view of mankind in the twenty-first century.

O people, come and breathe heavenly breaths! O people, run away from Shaytan and his representatives! All their advertisements, take them down and crush them, break them and burn them. Leave poisoned breaths! Come to breathe living breaths that are heavenly breaths. *Alhamdulillah!* Therefore, I am asking for me, for my brothers or sisters in Allah's way, "O my Lord, give us a day full of the pleasure of Your obedience."

For the honour of the most honoured one in His Divine Presence, Sayyidina Muhammad ﷺ—*Fateha!* ▲

9

CONCERNING MEN AND WOMEN

A'udhu bil-Lahi min ash-Shaytani-r-rajeem. Bismillahi-r-Rahmani-r-Raheem. La hawla wa la quwwata illa bil-Lahi-l-'Aliyi-l-'Azheem.

Life is the biggest grant from Allah Almighty to everyone. Even ants know this, and they are praising and glorifying their Lord. Ants and so many creatures smaller than ants, also, have an understanding, *idrak*.[67] They have an understanding, because you can't find anything in existence not knowing its Creator. It is open for all.

And that is what Allah Almighty is declaring in His holy books, particularly in the Seal of the Prophets' Book, the Holy Qur'an: *"Wa in min shayyin illa yusabbihu bi-hamdihi"*;[68] there is nothing in existence that does not know its Creator, knowing and glorifying and giving its thanks and praise to the limit of its level.

---

[67] Perception, awareness, consciousness, discernment.

[68] *"And there is not a thing but that it exalts [its Lord] with His praise."* (17:44)

If they have a level that they can reach and through it they can glorify, they are not leaving it. They are at their top limit of being in creation, and from that position they are giving their most high respect and praise and glory to their Lord. Everyone is giving it. Must be! *"Wa lakin la tafqahuna tasbihim,"*[69] but among mankind, not everyone can understand that secret and hidden position of each creature. Yes; nothing can be in existence without knowing and glorifying its Creator—*everything!*

Because it is an honour, you can't measure it, you can't bring a scale for the value of that honour. It is impossible to bring a scale for the honour that even a particle of an atom knows and feels, because everything that you bring as a measure belongs to our material world. No scale of the material world's values can give the amount of value of an atom's pleasure and feelings from being in existence. They just know it, and they are praising and glorifying.

What about man, mankind? The first man's design and form were just granted by his Creator. The Creator designed man, and then He gave his form *bidh-dhat*,[70] by His Own Self, not leaving it to the angels to do that; no. He designed and formed the first man as He liked, and also the first woman.

Men and women, they may seem so close in their designs, glory be to Allah, but they are not the same. Perhaps male and female, men and women, are just a hundred per

---

[69] *"And yet ye understand not how they declare His glory!"* (17:44), the continuation of the verse quoted in footnote 68.

[70] See 15:28-29; 32:7, 9; 38:71-72, 75

cent different. Their designs are a hundred per cent different; their forms, according to their designs, are a hundred per cent different. Even a hair on the bodies of men and women is different, a hundred per cent. Their outward design is a hundred per cent different; their inner organs are a hundred per cent different from each other. They are a pair and from the outside you think that they are similar, but they are not similar. They are a hundred per cent different.

And Shaytan, in his foolishness and idiocy, is running after heedless mankind and trying to make men and women understand that they are same. They are saying, "Equality between men and women!" *Yahu*, if there is equality, men and women must be only men or must be only women. If men are equal to women in everything, we must be women, not men. And shaytanic teachings are giving such a false understanding that men are like women or women are like men.

Satanic teachings are trying to make people's understanding about men and women like a caricature. A caricature is the simplest depiction of a person. If you think that this caricature is of that man, what is the distance between that man and his caricature? It is so distant that if that caricature is of a man, women are like men, or if that caricature is of a woman, men are like women, *that* far distant!

Allah Almighty is the Creator, *subhanallah*, first creating man, then creating woman. He is also the Designer and the Former, forming the first woman as He designed and formed the first man. Yet, although the same *mu'amala*, operation, took place, it was not like the first man's designing and creation. The Lord of Heavens is saying, "*Huwa-l-ladhi yusawwirukum fil-arham;*[71] I am the designer of you, O children of Adam, in the wombs of your mothers. I am that One. No one can involve himself in My designing and forming and creating and operating and granting what I am going to grant to that new creation of mankind in their wombs. *I am that One!*"

He created the first man outside because first man did not come from a father and mother. He prepared the design and blew into it from His Divine Soul. When that Divine Breath reached Adam, he got up and was ready to be a man, to be the deputy of his Creator.

Adam's creation was open, but Eve's creation was secret, hidden. Through traditional knowledge, we know that she was created from one of Adam's left side ribs but we are not given details. Adam slept a little bit, *sina,* took a little nap, and during that time Hawwa was created, ready. For Eve, Allah Almighty did not use what He used for Adam's creation, so many kinds of things to form him. Only a nap, and she was ready.

Therefore, women's creation is just a hundred per cent different from men's creation and their designs are a hundred per cent different from men's design. Traditional knowledge says that the rib bone from which Eve was formed was taken from the chest bone of Adam. Therefore, there is a area in men with no ribs. But what about for Hawwa, for women? Do they still have that *naqis,*[72] missing, rib?

---

[71]*"It is He who forms you in the wombs [as He wills]."* (3:6)
[72]Incompleteness.

Doctor, is it the same in women, also? I am asking if that bone is the same as in men.

[The doctor replies in the affirmative.] I know! I am saying that traditional knowledge says that that rib was just taken from us [men]. Therefore, there is a space, *naqis*. But what about women? Why is it continuing?

This is a secret knowledge that Allah Almighty is showing for our heedless understanding, that *I* created from it. And no one witnessed that creation and that happening. Therefore, women's spirituality is so high. Man's spirituality is so heavy. And women may quickly reach the highest positions in the Divine Presence; their souls are just prepared for that purpose. Therefore, women are closer to heavenly positions. Understand?

And the faces of heavenly beings always look, in their beauty not like men's but like women's beauty. *Tajalli*, the divine manifestation, just came at that point of creation when Allah Almighty was creating Eve from Adam's rib. Therefore, when Adam awoke and looked around, he had lost interest in everything in Paradise; nothing to look at and nothing to *taladhudh*,[73] to enjoy himself with. He was only attracted by the beauty of Eve. And beauty belongs to the Heavens and beauty is a grant from the spiritual world.

Therefore Rasul-Allah[74] was saying, "I like women, I love them. Allah is making me love them because their spirituality is so high, reaching heavenly positions, the spiri-

---

[73] To be sweet, delightful, pleasant, gratify the senses.

[74] The Holy Prophet said, "Perfume and women have been made dear to me, but the coolness of my eyes is in prayer." *(Mishkat)*

tual world."[75] This is something secret that you have never yet heard, anyone. And therefore women are in a position of respect everywhere. You may be a king, you may be an emperor. If a maiden comes in front of him with her beauty, he may come down from his throne and respect her, and his heart will go to her heart with love, with enjoyment.

A king enjoys nothing of the material beauties in his palace, as Adam did not enjoy himself with Paradise's grants. And he was walking up and down in Paradise as if he wanted someone else; his heart was not in satisfaction. Everything, every beauty in Paradise—jewels, gold, diamonds, palaces, everything—did not fill his heart with pleasure. But when Eve was sitting in her beauty, then Adam was saying . . . [pause; laughter]. Hawwa, Eve, was saying . . . [another pause, more laughter]. Therefore, it is not correct for women to run after men, but men must run after women. *Allahu Akbar!*

People in our time are learning only external measures for everything, never asking to enter into the real wisdom of things, into their true situations. They are measuring everything from outside, never entering into it. Therefore, Allah Almighty sent prophets to take people inside, to call to them, "Come in. Don't look too much at the outside of this palace, but come in and see what is in it."

They may reach heavenly stations so quickly, women. And we see, every time, that women go to spirituality more than men, and men are mostly like rocks or wood or without sense—so hard a creation, men! And the Lord just created men in such a way because the heavy burden of this life can't be carried by a creation like that of women. Therefore, men have been created with such hard characteristics, and it is very difficult to call men to be interested in spirituality, to leave material being and to run to their spiritual positions.

When, where, can you say that there is equality between men and women? Such foolishness, such foolish people! For what? To grind women, to make women like men. It is fighting against nature! You are finishing women spiritually and making them fade away if you use them for men's work or for what men have been made *mukallaf*,[76] what men have been ordered to do or responsibility given to them. The responsibility of men is all heavy work, to carry the heavy conditions of life as a shell protects a pearl. A pearl can't protect itself except by being in a shell, and men are like a shell for women. But they want to make the pearl like a shell.[77]

How can a shell be equal to a pearl? With what mentality are they claiming this and making so many noisy statements? And it is impossible!

---

[76]Responsible, authorized, commissioned, charged.

[77]Here, Shaykh Nazim adds humorously, "Eh, you may find a shell in the Shell Company. [Laughter.] You men go to the Shell Company. Say, 'This company owns us. We are shells! Give us our shares. Each year you get trillions in the name of Shell Company Oil.' You must make an application for the rights of mankind to ask for your shares from the Shell Company. [Laughter.] Yes. Why not? I shall write a application to make whole world stand up and ask for shares from the Shell Company!"

May Allah Almighty give us a good understanding, to give all our thanks to Him that He granted men what He granted, and granted also to women what men do not reach. But Allah Almighty granted women to be for men, also. Therefore, the Prophet ﷺ was saying, "Allah Almighty has made me love women," because each one of them carries a secret beauty from Beauty Oceans. That gives the hearts of men pleasure, and gives them the taste and pleasure and enjoyment of eternity. And in eternity, women are the whole of Beauty Oceans, to run in and be in. If no women, no Beauty Oceans could reach men.

May Allah forgive us! Be respectful to your wives, to women. Protect them and give them their honour. The twenty-first century's people are not giving real, true rights and respect and love to women, and they are wrong. Therefore, Allah Almighty is going to punish the twenty-first century's men by being killed most. If forty men are sent to death, there should be forty women for one man. Forty men are going to die and one man will remain, and forty times more women are going to be protected on earth. And those men who remain, they are those who are respectful to women, putting them in a highly respected position, forty women and one man. Forty men are going to die because they did not respect women, they did not give their true rights and respect.

The twenty-first century's people, they are going to be punished by the death penalty. Whoever respects women, Beauty Oceans appearing and the sweetness of life coming through them; those people should remain, and others should be taken away because they are rubbish.

We are asking to be respectful to our ladies, to all women. That makes Allah Almighty happy. For the honour of the most honoured one in His Divine Presence, Sayyidina Muhammad ﷺ—*Fateha!*

Therefore, in order not to be unmarried, so-and-so is looking for such a woman. Being unmarried is disliked in the Divine Presence. Allah never likes a person to be without marriage. You ask, Allah will send!

[To the ladies:] This is coming from Grandshaykh to give you honour. Some men are thinking that they will have forty wives. No, forty sticks! ▲

10

CONCERNING PREGNANCY, CHILDBIRTH AND NURSING

A'udhu bil-Lahi min ash-Shaytani-r-rajeem. Bismillahi-r-Rahmani-r-Raheem. La hawla wa la quwwata illa bil-Lahi-l-'Aliyi-l-'Azheem.

People think that their lives depend on food, they think that they are not going to live if not drinking or eating, That is really imagination. *Subhanallah,* glory be to the Lord of the Heavens, people have such imaginings!

Does a child in the womb of its mother eat or drink anything? No. It never uses its mouth to drink or to eat. But it grows till three times forty days pass. When it is four months and ten days, that piece of flesh changes and becomes another being.[78] Its organs begin to move, to act. And the *sultan* of the body, which is its heart, begins to pump, pumping, pumping, but still that that baby does not eat or drink. Every organ is okay and growing, growing.

---

[78] The states of creation of the fetus in the womb are mentioned in Qur'an, 22:05, 23:14, 40:67, 75:38.

In the womb of its mother, life begins, and the child grows without eating and drinking, not using its digestive organs. There is only a relationship to his mother, but that baby has no need to use its mouth for eating and drinking. No need for breathing, and it is in a bag full of water. Yes?

And when the Lord's command comes, those angels in charge of the baby make that child to be in perfect form and with its own special design in no more than nine months or ten days, maybe ten months, may even be eleven months, may even be twelve months, as He likes. That baby that is created in its mother's womb is not to be there for all time but it has a time that only He knows—the birth time, the time to come out.

Now, because of the foolishness of people, particularly physicians, they are doing something that is not for them to do, to be involved in the creation of that new one in his or her mother's womb. It is not for anyone to be involved, and to look and to say, "This is wrong, that is right. This is the opposite; that is better. This is an illness; that is healthy or ill." It is not for them.

And it is also not for them to say to people, "Your pregnancy has reached perfection, full-term. If you do not give birth soon, it will harm the baby and his mum," making the parents afraid. And they say, "Everything is okay, and the third of February," for example, "you must come in and we will take the baby from you."

By force? How can you take it by force? Did you create it? Do you think that if a person comes to a factory that makes cars and says, "This car is okay, I can take it," he will be allowed to do so? The one responsible for that factory will say, "Yes, it is finished, but approval must be there for each one before it goes out."

If the person says, "No. I don't need that. I must take it out because it is now okay. I must take it out by force," do you think that he can take it, the chief engineer or the manager giving permission to him to take it out? He can't give it. He must say, "Lastly, we must give our approval that it is a hundred per cent ready to go out."

Now, you can't take out a factory's car. Then what is this foolishness for doctors, physicians, to say to a pregnant women and her husband, "We must take it now because it is just perfect"? Where is the approval? You know that it is perfect? You are only looking at the calendar and saying, "You must take it now. If not, that new baby may die, and his mum, also." From where are you taking the authority to say, to claim this? But people are drunk, no-mind people. They believe in doctors, physicians, not believing in Allah.

When a baby is in the womb and the last approval has been made by the heavenly beings who are preparing and creating that new baby, the Lord of Heavens sends two angels. "Now that My servant is ready to leave the womb of his mum and come out, look there."

They look at the Preserved Tablet.[79] On the date on which divine approval comes, two angels come and they begin to take out that new servant of the Lord. One angel comes from one side, the right hand, and the second from the left hand. But that new creation, he is so happy in the

---

[79]The heavenly record of all of Allah Almighty's decrees for all eternity.

womb of his mother, and now he looks and sees his destination. He looks and sees what is really going to happen or what is going on in this world, and he does not want to come out. He is so happy in his mum's womb!

But he *must* come. One angel goes to catch him but he goes in another direction, and when the second wants to catch him, he goes there, till the angels say, "O our Lord, Your servant is making us tired and we aren't able to take him out. We have finished. Our power is not enough to take him or her out."

Then Allah Almighty says, "Leave!" And that new baby looks up, and his Lord, his Creator, *yatajjala*, gives a divine manifestation to that new creature, such a divine manifestation that he isn't able to stand up but just falls into *sajdah*,[80] prostrating to his Lord's glory and greatness, and at that moment he gets out. Therefore, during his or her birth everyone must prostrate to his Lord, making *sajdah*, and in that moment he easily gets out.

Not even angels are able to get him out. But our drunk doctors are cutting and taking out.[81] Who gives that authority to man to be involved? But people are also so foolish, becoming drunk, leaving their wives in the hands of such drunk physicians, to do everything to their wives. It is the biggest, biggest sin of man to involve himself in the creation of mankind!

---

[80]Prostration.

[81]Referring to the fact that Caeserian section births are very common in Cyprus and other parts of the world.

And that one; the new one comes, comes, *subhanallah*, glory be to Allah! He was in a bag full of water, and when he comes, the midwife makes some movements over him and he begins to breathe.

Subhanallah! When beginning to breathe, life runs through his body, everywhere. Without drinking and eating through his mouth, at that time he begins to breathe and wants something to use his mouth for. And he can only drink because his mouth is not yet ready with teeth for food. He only needs to suck at his mum's breast, *subhanallah!*

We were saying that people think their lives depend on eating and drinking. Yes—that baby comes and begins to take his mum's breast and drinks milk. Milk is one kind of food, and that baby drinks that milk and begins to grow from that one kind of food. The Lord of Heavens, the Creator, gives life to that child, and however many organs there are, inside or outside, each one makes another kind of cells from same thing.

How many kinds of cells do we have in our body? Hundreds? Hundreds of kinds of cells, nourished only by that milk. From milk, how does that baby open and grow, all its organs, everything—brain, eyes, ears, mouth and tongue, hands; and inside, heart, liver, lungs, stomach, intestines—growing from milk.

What is your proof? You can think about it. A person grows up to two years only drinking, and everything grows. Then he changes and tastes something by eating food.

Do you think that that milk makes that new baby grow? First, he was drinking and eating together. A new creation in the womb, what does he drink and eat? His food is through blood, blood from his mum, making him grow in her womb. We were once in that state, yes. Then, when coming out, red food finishes; changing to white food, to a white drink, and that drink makes him grow. Do you think that that milk has such power? If the heavenly order, heavenly command from the Creator does not come, who is going to grow in the womb of his mum or after birth?

Then we grow, we begin to eat and drink. Do you think that that drinking and eating is enough for you to move and do such things? What food can give you such energy that you are able to move around for twenty-four hours? Do you think that if you give a hungry person who is going to die a cup of milk or a pot of soup, drinking a cup of milk or a pot of soup will make him stand up?

What is in it? Doctor are saying, "Calories." What are calories? That one pot of soup, how does it give a person who may be one hundred kilograms, eighty kilograms, sixty kilograms—what does that one pot of soup do to make such a heavy person move? How?

People do not think about it. They say that we eat and drink and live. But that is false. If there is no connection, which is our soul and its spirituality, running through your body, even if you drank a big potful (like the curry pot of Pakistani people), you wouldn't be able to move—you wouldn't be able to move! But still they are denying what is beyond material aspects, not saying that there is something else that makes men use small amounts of material things, of material food, and that they are supported by spirituality. Otherwise, they couldn't move.

An example is coming now. It is like putting one litre of petrol into a a car. But if the spark plug is not there, what is the benefit of that petrol? This secret power is through that spark plug. If it does not give its secret power, that petrol does nothing. Therefore, if there does not come something from Heavens that belongs to our secret being like a spark plug, even if you eat a big pot of curry or soup, it is nothing. Understand? If you eat so many *tekerlek*,[82] so many cheeses like cars' tires, you can't move.

You must look and understand some wisdoms. A car can't move if the spark plug is not there. Burning—how does it burn petrol and then use it? Without that, it is impossible. If no involvement, if no connection to Heavens, no one can move on earth—never! If you put a car into a pool of petrol but the spark plug is not there, it can't move.

You understand? That is secret. Therefore, those who know this, they may take enough spirituality when they drink and eat. If not, they are like a car that has fallen into a pool of petrol but can't move, can't move.

Perhaps you must try to make roads, highways, *autobahns* for such cars, only to run on down below. But to go up, no! Therefore, if people do not use their spirituality, their lives are always running downward. They can't look up. They are always asking to move downward because they see that their movements are in a down direction, never asking to go up.

And there is special way, a special way for planes. Their sparks are of another kind, another power. Those who want to move up must use a different way to get up, very

---

[82]Tr., wheels.

powerful. If they do not use it and they use a simple relationship to Heavens, they may only move on the surface of this planet but not go up.

Therefore, all *anbiya*, prophets, and saints have such power to go up. Some people can move on the surface of this planet, but the majority are asking to run downward because they are not using a spark plug. They have fuel, they have petrol, but not that spark. Therefore, men are in need of heavenly sparks. If not, they are going to be rubbish. No value for them here or Hereafter.

May Allah forgive me and give you a good understanding and bless you. For the honour of the most honoured one in His Divine Presence, Sayyidina Muhammad ﷺ—*Fateha!* ▲

11

PRIDE IS ONLY FOR ALLAH

A'udhu bil-Lahi min ash-Shaytani-r-rajeem. Bismillahi-r-Rahmani-r-Raheem. La hawla wa la quwwata illa bil-Lahi-l-'Aliyi-l-'Azheem.

Have you ever seen an ant being proud over other ants? And an ant, if it is proud, what happens? Does its pride change it, does its pride do something to other ants?

O Fulan, you are a tall one. If your tallness, your height, was a reason to be proud, I think a camel would be enough. Its height is more than yours. And if you say, "I am taller than a camel," what about a *zarafa*, giraffe. A giraffe should be much prouder than you.

If you see that your weight gives you an authority to be proud, what about an ox? I think an ox may be four or five hundred kilograms or one thousand pounds. Eh, can you reach that weight? Do you think that weight is a reason for you to be proud? No.

If you have a reason for your pride, I think no wrestler can wrestle with a bear. Do you think that anyone can wrestle with a bear? What would happen? Do you think that your speed gives you a reason to be proud? Perhaps you can't catch up with a horse or even with a dog, even with a bear, even with a rabbit, or even with a kangaroo.

You know the kangaroo? Have you ever seen one? Champion; too speedy! A hundred yards, and its tongue becomes like this [panting]. But a rabbit going two hundred yards never does that. A rabbit—why not put a sign around its neck that it is so speedy an animal?

You are even proud of your flights, saying, "We are flying." No! What you made can fly but *you* can't fly. And man must blame himself: he can make an airplane, an instrument, to fly, but its maker can't fly. What is this foolishness? That material instrument is flying while its owner can't fly! If he can take a flight, he can fly with it, but by themselves, people can't fly. Why are we becoming proud that we made a flier, flying in the skies and reaching such far distances? A person must be ashamed that he is able to make a flier and that flier flies but its maker can't fly. But people do not think about it, and they are getting proud because of that instrument. He has no right to be proud that he invented and made a flying instrument from metal; it is not an honour for him. Perhaps he must be ashamed that I am making something that flies but I can't fly.

We are speaking about ants. Ants, they are not like mankind. They are not inventors, so if one of them is proud, it is not suitable for it because nothing is given to that ant to be proud of among others.

And we are looking at mankind. Everyone is made by the same manner of creation but they are in different designs and everyone's appearance is different from others'. And if one of mankind is proud because of his design, everyone has a reason to be proud because each person has a different, special design, a different creation, and no one else is made in that design. The Lord of Heavens makes mankind not to be proud of their outward aspects, of their designs, because your design is different from others' designs and everyone's value is different from others. No way or no chance for anyone to look at himself as being above others, no. It looks like the same design, but they are actually such different designs.

The worst characteristic of our egos is to be proud, and that was the reason for Satan's being cursed. He claimed that he was above the new creature, Adam. "I am above his creation," he was saying, looking at himself as being more perfect. He was thinking that his world was one world and Adam's world was another, and that Adam couldn't be above his world, where *he* was. That seeing himself as being above others or as being more valuable than others, looking at himself and his creation as higher than others' creations, that is an egoistical claim!

That is the first lesson for mankind: to learn and to know that pride makes a bad ending. You can do everything, but if you are a proud one, that pride carries you from the top level to the lowest level, the first lesson for mankind. Shaytan, Diabolo, was at the top point, in the station of *'izz,* honour, in the Divine Presence, but through his pride, he was just thrown down to the lowest level, falling down, the worst end for him. That was the first lesson, but I am sorry to say that, throughout the centuries, man is showing that bad characteristic.

And what happened to Shaytan is written in all holy books and mentioned in every message of Allah's messengers. From the first prophet to the last, it has been mentioned to mankind that Shaytan was thrown out of his honoured station to the lowest and most dishonoured station. Man is just deceived by Shaytan, and this, being proud, is a claim of our egos. Everyone's ego wants to be Number One; everyone's ego wants to be at the top point. No one wannts to be an ordinary servant. That ordinary servant is never going to be a proud one because servanthood tells you that you can't be a proud person because you are a servant. Pride is for your owner.

Who is your Owner? Your Owner is your Lord, your Creator, Allah Almighty. In His Divine Presence, if you claim, "I am proud," you are thrown out of servanthood. No!

Therefore, throughout the centuries, particularly during the Middle Ages in Europe, among all those who lived after Jesus Christ and Christianity had come to Europe, kings and emperors came on their knees when they were crowned, kneeling in front of bishops or popes to show that I am only a servant. Even if you put a crown on my head, still I am a servant of my Lord. And they thought or believed that holy people represented the Lord's honour and power on earth. Therefore, they came and fell on their knees, and that holy one in whom they believed put the crown on that prince or king or emperor. And they said, "We are only servants." It was good manners for those people who believed in God Almighty and were asking to be His servants.

When the big and most foolish, most crazy French revolution came, it finished those good manners, good teachings. It was such a big teaching to all mankind or to all their citizens that our king is accept servanthood to his Lord and coming on his knees with the crown on his head. It also gave a big lesson that, till you come on you knees and say, "O my Lord!" you are never going to be crowned, here or Hereafter.

Here, it is a grant from Allah Almighty for certain people to have a crown put on their heads—the lines of kings. It is also a proper line coming from Adam and Eve. That line has special aspects, a specialty for some of the children of Adam, as mentioned also among the twelve tribes of Sayyidina Ya'qub, Jacob's twelve sons. Among the twelve tribes, only one tribe was specialized to be kings. The tribe of Judah was specialized to be kings, just as Allah Almighty granted some of His servants' lines on earth to be prophets, and prophethood is a specialty for one line that came from Adam up to Sayyidina Muhammad ﷺ.

Not everyone is a prophet. A person may worship and he may do everything that he is able to do and he may reach the level of sainthood, but after sainthood he can't be a prophet. And therefore, also for kings, a servant may do his best service for his king but he is not going to be a king. Kings' lines are different.

Shaytan knows this. "If I can change it, I may collapse the whole world. I may carry them into a situation in which it is impossible to arrange their affairs, to bring solutions for their problems or to take away their troubles or miseries or sufferings." He knew this. Therefore, Shaytan did his worst, not his best, for mankind, and he stood up to take away emperors and kings, deceiving people, saying, "You must take them away. Kill them and shut that door so there will no longer come kings or queens or emperors. And *you* must be kings and emperors!"

They did that, and one of the most important supports against falling into a bottomless crisis in our days, it is only for that reason—that people followed Satan and took away their kings, queens, emperors and *sultans*, and they fell down, because to be *sultan*, to be king, to be emperor, that is a *takhsis*, specialty, from the Lord of Heavens. And you can now find some countries that are kingdoms, but those square-headed, no-mind people have just left kings or queens as a symbol, taking away every power from them.

When the big revolution, the French Revolution, came, it killed everyone from the line of those who were coming on their knees and saying, "O our Lord, this is Your grant on my head. And I am promising to keep myself as You like, to be a servant to You, O my Lord, and to keep Your orders as long as this crown is on my head." After that, do you think or do you know that any presidents or democratic leaders have come to a church and knelt down and taken that oath to their Lord? No. They are saying, "No"; they are saying, "No God! We are gods on earth."[83]

No! You are not gods but you are Nimrods. You are Nimrods! Therefore, this is the age of Nimrods, who say, "I am the Lord of the lands. O Abraham, where is your Lord about whom you say, 'He is in the skies'? Let Him come and fight me! I am ready to fight Him." In such a way now, everywhere, whoever comes to power thinks that he is a Nimrod.

Therefore, it is a point that is so important to be known. No way for humanity to bring real solutions to their prob-

---

[83]While in some nations the presidential oath of office is sworn on the Bible the essence of democratic ruling systems is secular and is not administered by a cleric but rather by a judge or other non-religious official.

lems until those foolish people stop saying "Democracy, democracy!" and making elections.

They are bringing a person from the mountains, from the jungles, and saying, "Sit down in the place of power. Use it as you like because so many million people are supporting you." What is this foolishness? That is a wrong system! Yet people are making elections in England, elections in Germany, elections in Sweden, elections in Italy, elections in Greece, elections in Turkey, elections in Cyprus, elections in Egypt.

Which elections? Look for the one elected by Heavens! Don't ask from the earth. Don't ask people to see, as they like, some person and give the center of power to him; no. You must look for the one who is elected by Heavens.

Therefore, finished! Now the whole world is full with wrong ideas, Satan dirtying their minds, also, and giving them this bad characteristic and saying to them, "You must be proud!" making their minds dirty. And *dunya*, the world, is just full of rubbish and it needs a cleaning. And now the cleaning is coming.

Keep yourself with truth. Therefore, we are saying, we are *haqqani*. That means truth supporters, truth seekers, truth defenders. That is our way. Those who are truth defenders, they are clean ones. If not, they are dirty people, rubbish; they should be taken away. We are asking for true ones who support truth, and truth comes from Heavens.

You can't know what is truth, O people, common people.[84] Be defenders of truth and look for true ones if you would like to be in an honoured station here and Hereafter.

May Allah forgive me and bless you with good understanding. For the honour of the most honoured one in His Divine Presence, Sayyidina Muhammad ﷺ—*Fateha!* ▲

---

[84]That is, those who have not reached the rank of "true ones"—that is, *awliya*, holy people or saints.

12

CONSIDER YOURSELF TO BE NOTHING

A'udhu bil-Lahi min ash-Shaytani-r-rajeem. Bismillahi-r-Rahmani-r-Raheem. La hawla wa la quwwata illa bil-Lahi-l-'Aliyi-l-'Azheem.

Y'attabir nafsik;[85] consider yourself nothing. *Lahiz nafsik;*[86] consider, you must consider. This is a very simple, very simple claim. Actually, we are nothing. *La mahala lil-'itirad.*[87] Really, we are nothing—not "to consider" but really, actually, we are nothing.

Yesterday we were nothing. Tomorrow we are going to be nothing. Between two nothings, how are we going to claim "I am here"? You understand?

How? Is it true or not? Yes, between two nothings, everything must be nothing. From nothing to nothing, if you make a bridge, that bridge is also nothing. That is a reality, a reality that perhaps a hundred per cent of people do

---

[85] Regard, consider, account yourself as nothing.
[86] Same as the preceding.
[87] There is no room for objection [to this statement].

not care about, rejecting it. And they are saying, "We are not nothing. We are *something*!"

Sometimes, from time to time, I go to the cemetery for a funeral. I am asking people buried there, "Oh! What about you? Where are you? If you were claiming, 'We are here, we are here,' where are you now? Where is your existence?

"Yesterday you were claiming that we are in existence, we are something. Now where are you? You were claiming this, but today, where are you, O people? You are now *really* nothing! Why were you claiming, when you walked on earth, that you were something? 'We are in existence. We are not accepting to be nothing.' But today you are nothing.

"Only one stone or some structure on your grave; but that is not your existence, that does not prove your existence. No; it is written on it 'John,' 'Jane,' 'Mary,' or this or that, she or he—so many words, but where is your *existence*? It is a label that is written on that stone, but that is not your existence, no. You have disappeared, you have finished. Now you are nothing. Why were you claiming that you had existence on earth?"

O people, why do you say this to others, because to claim that you are in existence is the source, the main source of troubles, main source of crises, main source of problems. It is a troublemaker, your ego, and your ego claims that it has existence. And as long as men claim that they are something, that trouble is never going to finish, wars are never going to finish, fighting is never going to finish, crises are never going to finish.

Shaytan was first teaching mankind and saying, "You are something," beginning to teach them, from the first level, that you are something. Then, "You are something more. You are something more than others."

Up to where does that reach? Up to the level at which Pharaoh, the Egyptian king, was saying, "I am your Lord," not being happy to be *something.* "'Something' is for ordinary people, but we are not 'something' like others. I am your Lord," he was saying, "the top, top level. *Ana Rabbukum al-'ala.*[88] I am everything; only *I* am in existence. All of you are under my feet, and whoever is under my feet, no existence for him."

Therefore, Nimrod was arguing with Sayyidina Ibrahim when Sayyidina Ibrahim said, "The Lord of Heavens gives life and takes life."[89] And Nimrod said, "Oh, I can do that, also. Bring me two slaves. One, I am now ordering his head to be cut off, killing him, and the second, I will not cut off his head, giving him life," reaching the point of saying, "Everything is under my control. I am your Lord and everyone is under my feet. You are my slaves. I may kill you, I may let you live."

The first lesson to mankind from satanic teachings is to *'ilqa*, throw, into their minds, "You are something. You must know that common people are rubbish. You must try to get out of being from common people, out of being rubbish. Then you should be *something*. Stand up and claim that!"

"How can I claim it?"

---

[88]"*I am your most exalted Lord.*" (79:24; also 26:28, 28:38)
[89]2:258.

"I will teach you, I will teach you!"

And Shaytan is teaching mankind. He has so many sciences. All sciences, he has been teaching, showing people. Inventions, they are all shaytanic, to make people find a reason to say, "I am something." And today, Shaytan's dominion is over the whole world, everywhere, saying, "You must study because by the way of studying you can be something, and more and more and more." Therefore, people are asking to reach a level at which they can say, "This is a degree." And as a rider hits his horse with his whip to reach its goal, Shaytan is urging people and hitting them with his whip to run after studying, saying, "You must try to study and to learn."

What are they learning? I am asking, "What have you learned?" Even graduated people are saying, "Nothing, but I have a degree, a Ph.D. I have a degree, but I never learned anything else. I only learned that I have a degree that *yumayiz*, distinguishes me from common people. With this diploma I have been distinguished from common people because common people are like herds. But we have graduated, we have degrees; we are not common people. We are no longer flocks, we are trying to be shepherds."[90]

---

[90]These comments relate primarily to higher studies in the Muslim world and other developing nations, where admission to universities departments is based on competitive entrance exams, those who score highest going to prestigious and lucrative fields such as medicine, engineering and law without regard for their suitability, interest or aptitude for such subjects.

Therefore, everywhere, everywhere—even my grandsons, from a young age—they are being made to go to school to learn. "They must learn."

I am asking, "What are they learning." [Chuckles.] They are learning nothing, but getting a degree. Degree people, what have you learned? They are saying, "Nothing, but we have a degree." Ah! Shaytanic teachings, everywhere!

This country, Cyprus, Turkish Cyprus, Northern Cyprus, has a handful of people. How many universities are there here? In a country with a handful of people, I think they are saying seven universities or ten higher education-schools and universities, and I heard that there are 20,000 students in those universities.

And universities, from the outside, you see them like a city, such big and attractive buildings, as churches are so beautiful, with such attractive architecture. You are looking—"Oh!" When you enter, you find nothing; coming, entering, going out, taking nothing. The outside attracts you, but inside, when you enter, you find nothing, only finding some candles and so many statues or paintings. And you lose yourself in looking at such beautiful paintings, like a person entering a museum, looking like this, like that, forgetting for what he has come in for. And finally they put a wax candle there and do like this, signing the cross on themselves, and going out but taking nothing. Their spirituality does not receive anything—no, nothing.

All universities now, everywhere they are building huge buildings so that if anyone looks from outside, he feels fear. "Such a university, how I can study in it?" giving a sense of fear and *istahiya*,[91] shyness. "How can I be here?" And when they open their books to learn, they learn nothing. Those are shaytanic tricks and shaytanic traps.

Oh, to study! For what? To reach a degree? For what? To prove their existence among his or her community; yes. "So-and-so, he is a Doctor of Architecture! So-and-so, he has a doctoral degree!" And foolish and heedless Muslims, they are also trying to reach a title, to be doctors from Sorbonne. They are not looking at Ahzar ash-Shareef,[92] that is really Islamic, with *'ulama*[93] there. They are going to Sorbonne or Cambridge or Oxford to get the title of 'Doctor,' and that proves to themselves that they are *something* in the community. And Shaytan is very happy.

First, Shaytan is doing like this for them [clapping], and this, at the level of studying, occupies young people in such a way. And then he is reaching people with a *çengel*, hook, to take them as supporters.

Shaytan wants to take supporters from top level people, also, and during thousands of years, he has worked on such a point that has opened for common people to be able to reach the power of a *sultan*, the power of a president, the power of a king. And they are teaching all people that these kingdoms, monarchies, are keeping you from the top level of proving that you are something.

"Only kings are saying, 'We are everything,' and you can't even say, 'We are *something*.' Why are you their servants? Why do you go down on your knees to them? Why

---

[91]Shame, shyness.

[92]Azhar University, Cairo.

[93]Islamic scholars.

do you give your respect to them? *You* must also reach that point."

"What shall we do?" people are asking.

Shaytan is saying, "You must remove kingdoms and empires and *sultans*. Then the whole country is going to be with you through election."

Election; yes. In olden times, sometimes they made an election; it is written about in books. Sometimes, when such funny people were running for election, they sent up a pigeon or a dove. If it came and landed on someone's head, they made him king or *sultan* over themselves. It was so much more honourable than these elections because a dove or pigeon did not make a *hile*, trick, no. But in their elections, they are making thousands and thousands of tricks and traps for people.[94]

Elections—very good! You can bring a person from the mountains, also. He has a chance to be President. Bring someone from the desert; he has a chance to be Prime Minister. Bring a market person, shouting "Potatoes, tomatoes, cabbage! Cheaper!" In England, yes? "Cheap! Finishing!"

"Come!"

---

[94] Here, Shaykh Nazim adds facetiously: "I am suggesting to all nations to do this, to use a pigeon. On whichever one it comes, finished. In Ireland, troubles should finish. When I was a young one they were fighting. Now I have become an old one and asking to leave this life, and they are still fighting. Why? Use a pigeon. Gather the people. On whomever it comes, Catholic or Anglican, it doesn't matter. Protestant, Jesuit—put him in; finished!"

"For what shall I come?"

"Come! You may write your name to be an M.P."

"Can it be?"

"Why not? You have that chance, also."

These are such nonsensical things that are just making all countries fall into bottomless problems and troubles. In Iraq now, clever ones want to make a federal system, with appointed ones. People are fighting now; they are saying, "No. We want elections." They learned that from Shaytan, because elections never bring suitable ones, always bringing unsuitable ones, always no-mind people, always square-headed people, always heedless people, always ignorant people. And Shaytan likes to make such troubles continue. If a federal system comes, it is stable. Everything is in its place, can't move, on a strong foundation, and people never like Shaytan and Shaytan's followers.

And in Islam, there are never going to be elections, never going to be democracy, never going to be a republic. They are all *batil*[95] in Islam. But our people, Muslims, they are also deceived by shaytanic teachings; shaytanic ideas are just running through the Muslim world, also. May Allah forgive us!

Therefore, we began today by saying that at least *sometimes* consider yourself to be nothing. If you do not really mean it, still say, "I am nothing." Don't trust degrees and don't trust common people's support. Don't believe com-

---

[95] Arabic: *batil*, False, baseless, vain, futile.

mon people. At any time they may take their support from you and you will fall down, never getting up, standing up—finished, so many people.

That is the main treatment for all people on earth now—for everyone to say, "I am nothing." When everyone accepts to say "I am nothing," they can improve and they are going to be supported by heavenly support. They are not in need of the support of people on earth. No; support from Heavens, no one can take it away. But people are deceived and they are asking for support from people. Support from people is like a candy cane for a building. A building can stand with it? Never! So many people are just falling down in such a way, deceived by Shaytan.

Therefore, O people, come and say, "I am nothing. I am only a servant created by the Lord of Heavens. I am His servant and my honour is to be His servant. His servanthood is my highest degree, highest honour." That will clean the whole world and make them victorious over evil and devils. If not, they are going to be ground up and finish.

May Allah forgive us and send His blessings for all nations to come and *'itiraf,* admit, truth and ask for true ones. For the honour of the most honoured one in His Divine Presence, Sayyidina Muhammad ﷺ—*Fateha!* ▲

13

OUR STOLEN DIAMONDS

A'udhu bil-Lahi min ash-Shaytani-r-rajeem. Bismillahi-r-Rahmani-r-Raheem. La hawla wa la quwwata illa bil-Lahi-l-'Aliyi-l-'Azheem.

This is an Association. It is not a lecture, it is not a university classroom. This place is a free place. We are trying to reach people's hearts, and that is the most important point—to reach people's hearts.

The most important point—and the mission of all the prophets concerned that point—is to reach to people's hearts and carry them to their Lord. As a *mithal,* example, if a thief steals something and runs away, the owner runs after him to save what he has taken and run away with.

Now, at the beginning of mankind, when Adam and Eve were sent down from Paradise to earth, Shaytan was also kicked down. And a warning came to Adam and Eve: "Beware of your enemy because he is running after you to steal what you have been granted from My Divine Presence."[96]

From that day on, Shaytan has been running after the children of Adam to steal what they were granted by their Lord, while he was prevented, he was not granted that honour. Then Shaytan was thinking and reaching everywhere to destroy everything for *Bani Adam*, the Children of Adam.

He wanted that honour to be granted to him, and when Allah Almighty did not grant it to him, he was very angry and began to argue in the Divine Presence. And Allah Almighty said, "Go away, demon![97] You are not one to argue in My Divine Presence. Kick him down, O angels!"

Falling down, falling down. And as a cat always lands on four feet, never upright, he turned like this and stood on the earth, and said, "I am here, also. O Adam, I will not let you and your children be at rest to taste that honour here, and I am going to try to take that honour from you. As I have been *mahrum*, deprived, of that honour, I will not let you taste that honour, either in this life or the next life."

Therefore, at his first step on earth, he declared war on Adam and his descendants. "I am that one who has come to steal that most precious grant from your Lord" — *edepsiz*,[98] not saying "*my* Lord"! "Your Lord's grant, I am going to

---

[96]See 2:36, 38; 7:11-27; 20:117, 123; 28:15; 35:6; 36:60; 43:62. Also see 2:168-169, 208; 6:142; 12:5; 17:53, 17:53; 18:50

[97]7:13, 18.

[98]Mannerless. This refers to 7:20, in which Shaytan, while urging Adam and Eve to eat from the forbidden tree, cunningly refers to Allah Almighty as *"your Lord,"* instead of "my Lord" or "our Lord."

steal it from you. I tried and I made it so that you were thrown down from Paradise to earth, also.

"Now you are innocent.⁹⁹ I can't do anything to you. But your children will not be innocent. Therefore, I shall try to do my worst to you and to your children, to make your heart drip blood from sorrow. I shall do this."¹⁰⁰ And from that day up to today, he has never tired or gotten fed-up, always with us everywhere.

I am asking so many people, Wahhabi people, also, "Do you think that the Prophet ﷺ is everywhere"

"O Shaykh, don't say that! *Shirk!*¹⁰¹ If you are saying that, it is *shirk*."

Another question to Wahhabi people: "What do you think about Shaytan? Do you think that there is any place where he is not present?"

They are surprised, astonished. "How can you ask this? He is everywhere!"

"Ah! For Shaytan to be everywhere is not *shirk*. But if the Prophet ﷺ is everywhere, *shirk*." [Laughter.] In such a way, you have been deceived by Shaytan.

---

⁹⁹Meaning that Adam and Eve had repented and were forgiven. Moreover, their sin was one of forgetfulness, not of deliberate disobedience.

¹⁰⁰4:118-120; 7:16-17; 15:39-40; 17:53, 62, 64; 18:50; 38:82-83.

¹⁰¹Arabic: *Shirk,* the greatest sin in Islam, that of ascribing divinity or its attributes to other than Allah. But according to Islamic belief, while prophets experience bodily death like all human beings, they are alive with Allah in the spiritual world.

Such wrong things from Arabs! Islam began with them, and then they became destroyers of Islam as the Last Days approached,. They are blaming us because of our beliefs, and I am saying to them, "We are *'ajam*,[102] we are not Arabs. You are Arabs, from around the Seal of the Prophets ﷺ, and taking from him and bringing to our places those books from which we are learning about beliefs. They are not from ourselves. Why are you now blaming Pakistani people, Afghan people, Turkish people and foreign people who are Muslims, and saying, 'All of you are on the wrong way'? Did we bring Islam or take it from you?"

In such a way, during the twentieth century, Arabs did their worst for Islam, and every curse that is now coming on them and from them to the whole Islamic world, they are responsible for it. We are not responsible, no. We are *Ahlus Sunnah wal-Jama'ah*,[103] never changing, but they are bringing accusations of "*Bid'a, bid'a*."[104]

"O Shaykh, if you say *salat wa salam*"—giving your best respect to the Prophet ﷺ by saying, "*As-salat wa-s-salam 'alayka, ya Rasul-Allah*," after the *adhan*[105]—they they are saying, "*Bid'a, bid'a!*"

"This *adhan* is just called for the honour of that Prophet! What does it do to you if I say, '*As-salat wa-s-salam 'alayka, ya*

---

[102] Arabic: *'ajam*, non-Arabs.

[103] Arabic: *Ahlus Sunnah wal-Jama'ah*, the people of the Prophet's *Sunnah* and Congregation, i.e., Sunni Muslims.

[104] Arabic: *Bid'a*, an innovation or something unprecedented in religion, a heretical doctrine or practice.

[105] That is, to observe the tradition of saying, "Peace and blessings be upon you, O Messenger of Allah," after the call to prayer.

Rasul-Allah'? Where do you find that it is *haram*[106] or *bid'a?"* They are *ahlu-l-bid'a!*[107]

But now they have reached ripeness, finished![108] If corn grows and gives ears, no matter how much water you give it, it does not grow more. Its final goal is the ear's coming into existence, and if you cut that ear, it will not grow again and bring another ear. That is their method. *They* are *ahlu-l-bid'a!*

But Islam is like a tree. *Y'uti ukulaha kulla hin.*[109] At every time, you can find fruits on that tree. If cutting the fruits, the tree is not going to go. The tree will live for the next year, to bring other fruits, more and more.

Then, Shaytan is reaching everywhere, and never getting fed-up and never getting to be tired, to steal what mankind have been granted by their Lord—the most precious jewel, diamond. And he is making thousands and thousands of tricks and putting thousand and thousand of traps for mankind to fall into and to steal it, *subhanallah!* And Allah Almighty sent the first man, Adam, as the first prophet, as the first advisor and *nadhir*, warner, to mankind, to say, "Beware of Shaytan!"

People are writing on their doors, "Beware of the dog." I am saying, "What is this? Why do you not write 'Beware

---

[106] Arabic: *haram*, prohibited, forbidden.

[107] Arabic: *ahlu-l-bid'a* , people of innovation. Those who create new forms of worship which have no bases in Islam.

[108] Meaning that such accusations cannot grow past the present level.

[109] *"It produces its fruit all the time."* (14:25)

of Shaytan'?" Always after dogs, "Beware of dogs, beware of dogs!" This *miskin*, poor, dog—what is it doing? And it is tied up, threatening people and sometimes attacking them, but people can defend themselves and escape. But I have never seen anyone writing, "Beware of Shaytan, beware of Diablo!"

That is the most important aspect, the most important point in the lives of mankind to know, to learn, and to try to protect themselves from Shaytan because Shaytan is running after everyone to steal his most precious diamond. Do you think that if thieves find a special and very expensive ring on a hand, they will leave it on that hand?

Satan is running behind, to steal everyone's diamond. And the Lord of Heavens sent to the children of Adam special people who are in connection with Heavens to save what has been stolen from them, their most precious diamonds That is the mission of all prophets, nothing else. Everything that prophets brought is a prevention or a protection for mankind so that their most precious jewel that is granted to them by Allah Almighty may not be stolen.

And the most important point now is to run after Satan and his armies and after devils, to take from them what they are stealing from man as they are stealing it and running away. All prophets tried to do this, but Shaytan and his assistants and agents and armies are always deceiving people and making them not look after such a precious diamond, making them forget it. And now all mankind, perhaps ninety-nine per cent, do not know that their most precious diamond has been stolen, no.

This is a humble meeting. We are trying to make people wake up—to see, to know, to recognize, and to ask, "What have we lost? Which thing has been stolen from us?" But it is such a humble meeting.

And you must be, everyone, helpers to prophets to be awake concerning Satan, not to let him steal your most precious diamond, and also to help people whose diamonds have been stolen. You must run to help people reach and take back their most precious grant that has been stolen by Shaytan and his descendants. To do that is the most honoured worship for the Lord of Heavens. He should be so happy and pleased with you.

Therefore, He is ordering, "O My servants, you must try to be with true ones.[110] Those true ones, if you are going to be with them, they may be able bring back to you your most precious diamond that has been stolen. Don't leave them!"

But now people have left true ones. They are following liars. We are *haqqani*; that means "truth defenders." We are defending truth and we are asking for true ones. And we are looking and seeing that the salvation of mankind, here and Hereafter, is to be with true ones and to be truth defenders.

May Allah forgive me and bless you. For the honour of the most honoured and most true one among mankind, Sayyidina Muhammad ﷺ—*Fateha!* ▲

---

[110] "... *Be with the true ones.*" (9:119)

14

SEEKING LIMITLESS LEVELS IN THE DIVINE PRESENCE

A'udhu bil-Lahi min ash-Shaytani-r-rajim. Bismillahi-r-Rahmani-r-Raheem. La hawla wa la quwwata illa bil-Lahi-l-'Aliyi-l-'Azheem.

[A peal of thunder. In keeping with the Prophet's *Sunnah*, Shaykh Nazim recites,] *"Wa yusabbihu-r-r'adu bi-hamdihi, wal-mala'ikatuhu min khifatihi. Wa Huwa 'ala kulli shayin qadir.* [111]

It is an Association, and Association helps people. If they are doing wrong or going in the wrong direction, it brings them to the right direction. Association helps pilgrims if they have lost their way in deserts, making them find their way to reach their goals.

---

[111] *"And the thunder exalts [Allah] with His praise, and the angels, due to fear of Him"* (13:13). *"And He is powerful over all things."* (2:20 and numeous other verses)

And *subhanallah—li kulli insan*, for every person, there is a goal. *"Subhana man 'auwana kulli qalbin ma yushghaluhu."*[112] Allah Almighty gives something to everyone's heart to think about and to want to reach his goal. Here, there may be a hundred persons. Everyone's heart goes in another direction, everyone thinks something different. It is impossible for two people's hearts to be on the same goal.

People may be occupied by trying to be an M.P. It is okay. If a hundred people or a thousand people want to be M.P.s, doesn't matter. But behind it, what they are suggesting is, "When I am an M.P., what am I thinking of doing, what is my goal by trying to be an M.P.?" Therefore, everyone's heart is just occupied by a different goal. That means that everyone has some goal to reach and everyone is trying to find a way to his goal.

Now, we are simple servants, and we are like people wandering in a huge desert, scattered, not knowing. All these people are finding themselves in that huge desert—hundreds, thousands, millions and billions of people, coming together and asking, "What are we going to do?"

Therefore, the Lord of Heavens is sending to those wandering people and calling them, "Come! O people, come and join with Me or with My followers. We shall take you to your true goal," because goals are real, true ones or imitation ones. Calling them, "Come with Us! We shall take you out of this huge desert to your true goals, true aspects."

---

[112]Glory be to Him who supports every heart in doing that which preoccupies it.

As we said, everyone thinks something about the true, real goals that belong to our real being. Our real being, our spirituality, will never vanish or finish. And our goals, also, real goals, are never going to be lost or stolen, never going to lose their value. They belong to eternal life, up to eternity.

But the imitation goals that most people now are running after, those belong to our physical being, and our physical being enjoys itself when it reaches such cheap and imitation goals. Therefore, people's feelings are making them run toward those goals because their physical beings' five senses are just in touch with their imitation goals.

Real goals are beyond their goals. First, they are getting in touch with their physical beings' wishes, their physical desires, and they are thinking that the real desire or real aim of their being is to reach those goals. That means physical desires. And when you say, "O people, beware! O people, don't be deceived, because you are not the first ones who have lost those cheap goals, imitation goals," quickly, when their physical being is destroyed and finishes, they find that they have reached nothing because our physical being's goal and pleasure is in fulfilling physical desires. But from the age of majority, it begins to become less, less, less, less, till coming to the point of zero.

They are looking and seeing that, but shaytanic advertising, shaytanic teachings, are always deceiving mankind and saying, "No! You must continue on that way to reach your never-ending desires," promising them to reach the fulfillment of never-ending desires. But finally, at their last breath, their mouth open and their eyes closing, at that time they understand that they have been cheated. At that moment, they understand that they have lost everything; at that time they understand that they have reached zero, nothing.

But no chance for them to come back again for a new beginning. Such people, even if they were to be brought here again, they would do the same thing. If asking a third time to come and reach the real aspects of their life, their physical desires and five senses would just occupy them and close down the lights in their minds and extinguish the lights of faith in their hearts so they wouldn't be able to see real goals, because material aspects and physical desires are imprisoning souls, and souls aren't able to reach their real goals within that person.

And the Lord of Heavens sent us His chosen servants who are in connection with Heavens to remind His servants, "O people, you must not be deceived by looking at imitation goals as a permanent enjoyment, a permanent aspect for yourself, but you must come and look at your real aspects in this life so that you will find your real goals in Heavens, not on earth."

Those who are asking and trying to find their real goals on earth, they are going to be rubbish. Finally, they are going be dust, and their souls are going to be imprisoned in the darkest of dark worlds because they will be closer to the areas of darkness, the worlds of darkness, when they are under the earth. They should be imprisoned, their physical being dust and their souls imprisoned in dark worlds under the earth, those who are running after imitation and temporary goals.

Therefore, Allah Almighty sent His chosen ones to make people know this point and to show them the ways of Heavens, and all religions are showing the ways to Heavens. And in the Heavens, *tariqahs*[113] are different ways and lines for people. According to their ability or capacity or their inner manifestation, they should reach different levels in the Heavens.

And the number of levels in the Heavens has no limits—unlimited, no end, no final position for mankind. Each time a person asks for more, he should be granted more because those are the real, true goals that belong to our souls, and our souls will never vanish or finish. But our physical being is going to be dust, buried underground and finishing. And the souls of the people whose goals were on earth should be imprisoned in *Sijjeen*;[114] they should be there.

And those who are asking for real, true goals that belong to their souls, they should reach, one after another, unlimited levels in the Divine Presence. According to their servanthood, they should be more and more pleased and in pleasure, and they should swim, they should dive, into streams of light, reaching unlimited Light Oceans. And Allah Almighty grants all kinds of Oceans that have no limits to His servants who keep His glorious service in His Divine Presence. They should be under His divine dominion for eternity, and nothing can describe their honour by being servants of the Lord of Heavens, whose dominion no one knows.

Therefore, the Lord of Heavens wants to make His servants come to Him. *"Wal-Lahu yad'ua ila dari-s-salam."*[115] "Come to Me!" Allah Almighty is saying. "I am inviting

---

[113] Sufi orders.

[114] The lowest depths of Hell, mentioned in 83:7-8.

[115] *"And Allah invites to the Home of Peace."* (10:25)

you to Me, to Me, to Me, to Me! You should find Me; if you are asking for Me, you should find Me. Whoever finds Me, he is for Me. And My Mercy Oceans, Light Oceans and countless Glory Oceans under My divine dominion, they should be for you, free for you, because you chose Me and wanted Me, and I accepted you. You should be for Me. You sacrificed your existence, and finished. You are under My divine dominion's Oceans."

No finding *"Ana, anta.*[116] I am here, You are there"; no. It is *maqam fana fil-Lah* and *fani fil-Lah* and *baqi bil-Lah*. That person sacrificed himself, and Allah Almighty grants him from His divine blessings that make that one be with Him, under His unknown dominions, never-ending Blessing Oceans, never-ending Beauty Oceans, never-ending Mercy Oceans, never-ending, never-ending, never-ending Oceans, Oceans, Oceans, countless Oceans!

That is the goal, not this world's rubbish. But people are just deceived by Satan, and they are running after rubbish and running to the dustbin to look, to find something, while the *Sultan* is inviting them: "Come to Me! I shall give you something that no one has seen, no one heard of, no one knows."[117]

But people are saying, "No, we are not in need of that. We are looking in the dustbin, what there is to take." And they have lost their ways and they have lost what they should be granted by their Lord.

---

[116] "I, You."

[117] See Qur'an, 32:17; Bukhari, 6:303; Muslim, 363, 6783.

May Allah forgive us and send us some of His real guides to find our way to our real goal. For the honour of most honoured one in His Divine Presence, Sayyidina Muhammad ﷺ—*Fateha!* ▲

15

ABOUT BEING TRUTH DEFENDERS

A'udhu bil-Lahi min ash-Shaytani-r-rajeem. Bismillahi-r-Rahmani-r-Raheem. La hawla wa la quwwata illa bil-Lahi-l-'Aliyi-l-'Azheem.

That lamp is a good lamp. Why? It shines. If it does not shine, we will throw it away, useless; we will not keep it inside. It will be useless because it does not shine, throwing it in the dustbin. And mankind now, all of them who are shining should be accepted. If not shining, they will be thrown away in the dustbin.

And Allah Almighty is saying, "I sent to you, O mankind, from My divine lights from Heavens. Why are you not taking them—*why?* Coming to Me without shining, without lights? Take this and put it in the dustbin!"

That was the mission of all prophets. They brought heavenly lights because men are in darkness here; they need lights. Those who are escaping from lights, they are running after Shaytan, and Shaytan and his followers must be thrown into darkness, dark worlds. Shining worlds and dark worlds—Heavens are full of lights and dark worlds are in darkness. You can choose your way.

Therefore, Allah Almighty was saying to His Prophet ﷺ, "O My beloved one, don't be worried about people or don't force them;[118] don't force them to accept what you are bringing. If they do not see light and darkness, leave them. I like those who accept what I am sending of lights. Whoever accepts My gift of lights, that one is for Me. If they do not prefer or choose lights, heavenly lights, leave them. They have dark worlds. I will send them there."

And underground, so many, so many *hasharat*, insects, live in darkness and they are happy there. If you bring them out, forcing them to come out, they can't live, no; they don't like it. Therefore, leave them. If they prefer or choose to be like spiders or scorpions or forty-legged insects and so many other *hasharat*, leave them. Don't run after them because they are such foolish ones.

"They are not *takdir etmek*, appreciating, My grants to them. I granted them minds, but My biggest grant to them, to mankind, that I never gave to other creatures, is will. I have not given it to anyone else."

Even angels have no will. Angels are fully, one hundred per cent intelligent creations, but without will. They are under His will, never coming out. And the animal world's members were not granted will or mind. But mankind have been granted minds to think, to know, to learn, and then to do.

To do anything, you need will, and Allah Almighty granted us will so that we may choose anything we like. And He put in front of mankind so many things so that they may prefer one of them, good things or bad things.

---

[118]See 3:176; 5:41 [5:44 in Yusuf Ali's translation]; 7:188; 10:65, 99; 36:76.

You may drink water, you may drink whisky. It is for you to decide. The one who drinks water is using his mind and good will power, but those who drink drinks like whisky and other alcoholic drinks are not using their minds, and they are using their good will as a bad will and drinking.

It is forbidden. Anything that the Lord of Heavens has forbidden or made prohibited is for our benefit; finally, ultimately, we should be happy. But those who are not listening to what Allah Almighty is offering to them, they think that what is prohibited is a good thing but forbidden.

Nothing of the sort! The Lord of Heavens never makes something forbidden if it gives benefit to mankind. Say, Europeans, Americans, the most civilized people—can you say that Allah made some things forbidden while they were or are for the benefit of mankind? They can't say so! They must be drunk people to say that, and a drunk person is a no-mind person. What he is doing is all wrong.

Therefore, people to whom Allah Almighty, our Creator, our Lord, granted minds to think and will power to force our physical being to do or to make or to keep some rules, it is the biggest grant from Allah Almighty. And when prophets came, they were representatives of Heavens, coming and calling, "O people!" Only prophets said, "O people, use your minds! We are asking from you to use your minds, nothing else.

When people reach the age of maturity, they are not *mukallaf*, responsible, because at that age their minds are not perfect. Perfection begins at that age. Then Allah Almighty says, "O My servant, look! I have now granted you everything and you have reached the first step of your maturity.

Your mind is sufficient to understand what I have sent to you from My heavenly orders. I am saying to you, '*Aslim*. Surrender to Me, surrender to Me!'"

All prophets came and called people and said to them, "O people, come and surrender to your Lord."

And people were saying, "Oh-oh-oh-oh-oh! What is this? Who is that One that you are telling us we must surrender to? Where is He? We can't see Him."

"Eh, you can't see your Lord."

"We have so many idols, statues. We should ask them. If they say 'Yes,' we may follow you."

"Where are your idols? Coming from Heavens?"

"No. We are making, from stone, from wood, wooden idols, iron idols, and silver idols or golden idols or idols of jewels. We may ask them. If they say 'Yes,' we may surrender to you."

Oh-ho-ho! People are not using their minds. They are too drunk to think about such points. They are not free to think about it because they are busy, so busy. I am asking, "Why are you not thinking about it?"

And Americans are saying "No, no, Shaykh. We are very busy."

"With what?"

"Because we are doing research on Mars. We are researching what is there."

I am asking, "Have you finished with the earth so that you want to reach Mars? What is there?"

"No. We are so busy! No time for us to surrender to Someone. We want a free land like Mars. Nothing is there. We should be free! No one will call us, 'Come and surrender'—to be Jewish, to be Christian, to be Anglican, to be Orthodox, to be Catholic, to be Jesuit, to be Muslim. No one will ask us to surrender. We must run to *that* place!"

For a thousand years people have been thinking that there must be some live ones on Mars. Since centuries they were claiming that there are at least some live people, not close to our being but similar. "We must reach them to make them allies, to help us against the Chinese people [laughter] because they are so many, or against the Indian people; they are also one billion."

Finally, finally, they are making a competition. The Russians are saying, "We must hurry to land on it before the Americans. Why should the Americans put their flag on it? We must reach first, we must put our flag on it," and they are preparing to send their rocket. The Americans are very clever, waiting to see what will happen. And the Russians are saying that they needs three or four months to prepare.

Then going. When reaching there, because their brakes are not very strong, they can't land on it—destroyed! The Americans are looking. "Ah, we must be patient to see what happened to them. They disappeared. We must order our rocket, also, to land."

"Slow, slow; a smooth landing! When slowly landing, we will look." And they landed and said, "Oh-h, so happy!" But some of them were very sad. "We were expecting that they would come with their armies to make a parade because earth people have come to us," making a parade to welcome them. "None of them has come, no one!"

"Better! Perhaps they are afraid and running into caves. We must be very careful about that."

And they are running to be there, not to surrender to anyone but to be free, a hundred per cent free—a free land, free people, because on earth so many things are making them not to be free. No freedom on earth, and people are always saying, "O people, come and surrender."

"*There*, no one is calling us to surrender. We should be a hundred per cent free." And they are running there to be free, while on earth they were so unhappy because all the prophets were coming to them and saying, "O people, come and surrender!" And our egos never like to surrender.

When Allah created ego and asked it, "Who are you? Who am I?" its answer was "I am I, You are You," never saying, "I am Your weak servant and You are my Lord." The first argument just began at the beginning of our egos' creation, and it is continuing. Every time, our egos want freedom, freedom. That means no one is over us to ask us to surrender to Him and His orders.

That is the main reason why people are running away from religions, from faith, from beliefs. They are trying to change every religion according to their mind- productions, according to their minds, according to their physical desires. But every, *every*, belief from Heavens has come to make people surrender to their Lord, not to surrender to their egos, because ego is, in everyone, the representative of Shaytan, and Shaytan is never happy that people should surrender to their Lord and become His servants.

Shaytan wants to deceive people, and he is saying to them, "You must try to be free ones. Don't believe in anything with the name of religion or prophethood or holy books. Don't accept it! Instead, you must reject it and you must be free ones," until now they are the twenty-first century's people, running in the streets and roads, and demanding, "More freedom! More freedom!"

What, what? What should that more freedom be? For what are they asking? They do not know. They are shouting, making demonstrations everywhere and demanding more freedom, more freedom. What is "more freedom"? No one can understand, but Shaytan is making them demonstrate and make those never-ending troubles and problems on earth by always asking for freedom.

What more freedom should the government be able to give? What they are giving is in limits, also, because, after that limit, their own position is going to be in danger. Therefore, they are saying, "No. No more! You do everything you want, but don't come to us and say, 'We are asking for more freedom. You get down! We should sit there in your place.'"

All prophets came on the same point, to call people, saying, "O people, use your minds and surrender to your Creator, to your Lord. You should be good ones; you should be rewarded with a happy life, a peaceful life. When you surrender to His commands, you should be respected, you should be honoured." But people are never thinking about it.

I am very sorry when I see people in the streets. They are attacking and running in the streets and roads, and security forces are catching them and hitting them and carrying them by their legs and kicking them and doing everything bad to them. I am very sorry, because it is not correct for mankind to be in that position.

Arabs have a good saying, *"Ihtaram nafsak."*[119] You understand? I heard *"Ihtaram nafsak"* so much in Syria. *"Ihtaram nafsak"* means, "Keep your honour, O person!" If you do not keep your honour, then you may lose your honour because something may happen to you. If I curse you or hit you or kick you, it is not an honour for you. Keep your honour, keep your *namus*, dignity!

You are a noble one.[120] Don't put your nobility down among people, under their feet, under my feet or under someone else's feet. And so many people are carried to *garagol*, jail, and police stations. To be carried there, to be imprisoned, it is not an honour for them; to be kicked, to be hit, it is not an honour. Keep your honour, keep your respect from being touched, because you have been created as a respected one and the most honoured one among creatures. Why are you making yourself lose that respect? *That* is the reason.

Then, Allah Almighty is calling you to surrender to Him and you are refusing. You are losing your honour and respect. It is no good for you; you are not going to be a good one, no. People say that gangsters are the worst peo-

---

[119] Respect yourself.

[120] That is, enobled by being Allah's deputy with a special purpose and destiny.

ple. No honour for them, no mercy for them; they only look like men but they are wild animals. Don't be from among those people! Come and surrender to your Lord's divine service so that Allah gives you more honour and respect here and Hereafter.

Therefore, we are asking, "Who can say, 'I am a good one'?" If you surrender to the commands of your Lord, you are on the way to being a good one. If not, don't claim that I am good one—no.

Nothing of this world's aspects ever gives you the authority to claim that I am a good one—through your wealth, through your political positions among governments, through your business, through your gold, through any aspect of *dunya*. That never gives you the authority to claim that I am a good one; no. A person may be a worker and he may be a good one; a person may have the power of Nimrod but he may not be a good one.

May Allah forgive us and grant us good understanding. People from East and West are coming here now because now people are slowly understanding that they have been cheated by devils and Shaytan's tricks and traps. They are asking to save themselves from the hands of devils, bad ones, and to save themselves from their traps; they are beginning to ask. And Allah Almighty is going to change everything now, to take power from the hands of devils and to bring true ones.

We are here, claiming to be *haqqani*, truth defenders. I am not asking people to be English, to be Turkish, to be Pakistani, to be Arabs—no, nor white people, red people, black people, yellow people. It is not important. Now we are seeing who are going to be defenders of truth. We need such people now.

And people are running after true ones because they are fed-up with the lies of political people. The most lying people, they are! Therefore, people are now standing up a little bit, a little bit, getting awakened to ask, "Where are true ones?"

That is the safety or salvation of the world and all nations. Without true ones, this world is going to hells. Only true ones can stop it, and by taking the reins of life into their hands, they may stop it. Otherwise, this world is just going to fall into hells!

May Allah forgive us and quickly send us His holy ones! And you must be defenders of truth, not slaves of *dunya*, of Shaytan, of bad ones. May Allah forgive me and bless you! For the honour of the most honoured one, through His beloved one, Sayyidina Muhammad—*Fateha!* ▲

16

REGARDING THE STATE OF THE MUSLIM WORLD

A'udhu bil-Lahi min ash-Shaytani-r-rajeem. Bismillahi-r-Rahmani-r-Raheem. La hawla wa la quwwata illa bil-Lahi-l-'Aliyi-l-'Azheem.

Today I want to say something to our Turkish brothers—weekly advice, an Association for them. Tomorrow most of them are leaving *insha'Allah*[121] to Turkey.

Turks were for Islam like feet for a body, and Arabs were like the head. But a head without feet can't move. Therefore, for Muslim Arabs, Allah Almighty appointed Turkish people in Central Asia, and He prepared them for Islam. They accepted Islam and they did their best for Islam.

Up to 1924, Turks were Ottomans;[122] their real identity was Ottoman. Then the name of Ottomans was changed to

---

[121]God willing.

"Turkey" and "Turkish". Up to that time we were Ottomans, and the Ottoman Empire carried the holy flag of Sayyidina Muhammad ﷺ.[123] Then the Young Turks, who were called *Jöntürk*,[124] a new Turkish movement, caused the Ottoman Empire to finish, destroying the Empire and giving an imitation title, "Turkish Republic," to the Ottomans.[125]

And they accepted a secular system and put Islam aside. Since eighty years, they have cut their relationship with Islam a hundred per cent. Up to that time, Islam and its holy flag was carried by the Ottomans, who were Muslim Turks. Now Turkey is not saying, "We are a Muslim coun-

---

[122]That is, belonging to the Ottoman Empire, so named for Sultan Osman I, a thirteenth century Central Asian Turk.

[123]Referring to the Prophet's flag, which, together with other sacred relics of the Prophet ﷺ, is housed in Topkapı Museum in Istanbul.

[124]A group of Turkish 'progressives' of the early twentieth century who extolled nationalism and espoused the democratization and secularization of Turkey.

[125]Prior to 1924, there was no country known as Turkey. Anatolia, the Asian wing of what is now Turkey, and the European wing (Trakia or Thrace) were part of the Ottoman Empire, which included parts of the Balkans, Egypt, most of North Africa, Palestine, Iraq, and the Arabian peninsula. The Empire's sultan (ruler), headquartered in Istanbul, was at the same time its caliph (head of the Muslim *ummah*), and the Islamic *Shari'ah*, Islamic law, was the law of the Empire. However, after the end of World War I, under the influence of the forces of Turkish nationalism, the attraction of Europeanization and the desire for 'progress,' the caliphate and sultanate were abolished. The former Ottoman Empire was partitioned among the victorious allies of World War I and replaced by the present-day Republic of Turkey, together with the nation-states of Egypt, Libya, Morocco, Algeria, Tunisia, Jordan, Syria, Lebanon, Palestine, Saudi Arabia, Kuwait and the Arab Emirates.

try," but it is saying, "We have a secular system.[126] We no longer use the *Shari'ah*. We have a parliament now, and parliament makes the rules. *We* make those rules for our people."

This is really a *khuruj*, departure, from Islam, and they are sailing in an unknown direction. They do not know where they will end. Now, as the Turkish Republic, they are astonished. "Where is our destination?" They have departed from the Islamic territory and they are saying, "We are now sailing freely. We are now free from the *Shari'ah*, free from religious rules, free from the rules of the Holy Qur'an, free from the rules of Heavens. Now we are freely going across this ocean, anywhere we like." And now they do not know where they are going. What is their destination, they do not know.

Therefore, we are looking, and looking with wisdom, *'ibret*.[127] You must see where they are going, *they* do not know. Every year or two, or every month, they are changing their rulers, so that we may say their rulers are the new captains of their sailing vessel. Some people are saying, "We must go in this direction." And at the same time they are keeping the opposition people on that sailing boat, and they are saying, "No. We must move in *that* direction." Another party is saying, "No, this is the direction."

They haven't any compass, they haven't any map, they haven't any idea about any direction. They can just sail. They said only, "We must leave the harbour of Islam, we

---

[126] A clause in the constitution of Turkey states that secularism is the religion of the Turkish State.

[127] Lesson.

must go freely through this ocean. As we like, we may try any direction. Whatever we find, it is all right for us." And now they are turning around in that ocean. They do not know in which direction they will go or what is their destination. That is a big, big lesson for Turkish people, as well as for every nation that follows them.

Islam is stable. It has a stable base, a strong base. Islam is based on a heavenly base, but the new generations have rejected it, and they are now looking for a base and not finding it. And it is impossible to find. Finished!

We are saying that Allah Almighty just granted Islam to our ancestors in *ma wara'u-n-nahar*,[128] Central Asia. They accepted Islam with love and utmost respect. Perhaps no other nation respected and carried the holy flag of the Prophet ﷺ as they did. Those, our ancestors from Central Asia, carried it for one thousand years because Allah Almighty just appointed those Asian people, the ancestors of these Turkish people, as the 'feet' for Islam. And Islam spread and went on.

Those people who come from Anatolia now,[129] they know nothing because it is prohibited for them to know Islam. It is banned. Islam has been banned in Turkey since 1924. For sixty, seventy, eighty years, Islam has been

---

[128]Literally, "What is beyond the (Oxus) river," i.e., the Central Asian regions, known as Transoxiana.
[129]The Turkish mainland.

banned, and everything in the name of Islam is banned, also. And they did their worst for Islam.[130]

Now punishment is coming on them. Those who did that should be punished; they should be punished! Now the time is coming. And every nation among the Islamic nations, also.

First, Arabs are going to be punished because they first did *ihanet*,[131] putting Islam down and asking for another system. And Arabs know, through their language, that Allah Almighty is saying, "*Wa man lam yahkum bima anzala-Llahu, fa-ula'ika humu-l-kafirun*[132]—those who change *Shari'at-Allah*,[133] the holy rules that Allah sent to them from Heavens, they are unbelievers." Arabs know. They recite the Holy Qur'an,

The first believers were Arabs. The first unbelievers now are Arabs. It is not permissible for them to follow Europeans or Western people, and to change *Shari'at-Allah*, the holy commands and holy rules from Heavens, and to bring parliaments and elections—to do such foolishness.

Europeans and Western people can do that because in Christianity there are no rules for *dunya*, worldly affairs, and

---

[130] While a formal, limited version of Islam authorized by the Turkish government exists in Turkey, the expression of Islam's beliefs and the observance of its practices is surrounded by official limitations and prohibitions.

[131] Ar., *khiyana*, treachery, betrayal.

[132] "*And whoever does not judge by what Allah has revealed, then it is those who are the unbelievers.*" (5:44)

[133] *Shari'ah/Shari'at*, the sacred law of Islam, derived primarily from the Holy Qur'an and the Prophet's *Sunnah* (practice).

no rules for governments. But Allah Almighty sent to Muslims, to *ummati-Muhammad*, the nation of Sayyidina Muhammad ﷺ, such rules that no one can remove them from their centers. But first Arabs and then Turks removed them and brought a parliamentary system from the Europeans.

They are saying "Democracy!" No democracy in Islam! Democracy means that power should be in the hands of the people,[134] while Islam says that all power is in the hands of Allah Almighty. How can you do this?

Only Allah can do this! You are not allowed, you can't make laws, rules for people, no.[135] Only Allah Almighty can send them. He sent His *Shari'ah*, ruling His servants up to *Yaum ul-Qiyamah*, the Day of Resurrection.

Turks are saying, "Turkish Republic, secular system." But what about Iranian people? They are saying, "Iranian Islamic Republic." How can it be—*how?* Parliament means that people put the rules.

No rights for servants to make rules! Making rules is only for Allah. He can make rules for His servants; servants can't make their rules for themselves. What is this foolishness? And they are saying, "O-oh, Iranian Islamic Republic." *Masha'Allah!* Which book is writing this? How can that be?

---

[134]That is, legislating and judging according to the man-made notions of people rather than by the sacred laws revealed in the Qur'an by the divine Law-Giver and Ruler of the universe, and proclaimed and exemplified by His Last Prophet ﷺ.

[135]I.e., rules governing principles, values, morals, famly life, interpersonal and international relations, what is permissible and prohibited, etc.

And Arabs—so many republics and dictators among Arabs. How are they understanding? They are understanding that the feet are the head and the head is the feet. What is this foolishness, what is this *kufr*,[136] while Allah is saying, *"Wa man lam yahkum bima anzala-Llahu fa-ula'ika humu-l-kafirun;* those who do not obey heavenly rules, they are *kuffar*. They are not Muslims, they are not believers. I am not accepting anything from them till they leave that wrong way."

Poor Pakistani people, what should they say? [Chuckles.] Pakistani people are saying, "We do not understand Arabic, and we have brought Musharraf Khan or another Khan or another general to power." A general, what does he understand of the Holy Qur'an, what does he understand of the *Shari'ah*? He is a soldier, a general. What is this?

And so many *'ulama*[137] in Pakistan; so many groups—*Minhaj al-Islam, Tablighi Jama'at* and other groups, Muslim *jama'ats*,[138] so many *tariqahs*—all of them saying nothing, and a general comes and sits? What is this? What is the place of a general to come and be President? How can it be? They have an excuse because they are not Arabs. They do not know. But what about Egyptians, what about Libyans, what about so many Arab countries?

And foolish Pakistanis and other groups that are claiming, "We are Muslims," are defending the Dictator of Baghdad, Iraq, saying he is *mazhlum*, oppressed. How are you saying this? What is your proof? That person is also a gen-

---

[136]Unbelief, denial of truth. *Kuffar*—unbelievers.

[137]Islamic scholars.

[138]Groups, associations.

eral. What is his position in front of the *Shari'ah*? If the *Shari'ah* brought a case against them, calling them for judgment, all of them should be killed, should be thrown into Hells.

But this is the time of *fasad*.[139] The *khalifah*, caliph, has gone, and now they are asking Allah Almighty to help them. But Allah never helps a *zhalim*, an oppressor. *"In tansuru-Llah, yansurkum."*[140] Therefore, if other Muslims' punishment is one, Arabs' punishment is seven times, and *nar*, fire, is beginning to burn the *kufr* of Arabs, from Baghdad. All *awliya*, saints, are against them, and now everywhere there is coming the end of their periods, one by one. One by one they should be burned, till the Mehdi[141] comes.

American Muslims are saying, "We can never reach any power." Spanish people are saying that, also; Germans are saying it, also. No. They haven't any responsibility, but responsibility is, first of all, on Turks or Arabs, or on Arabs, then Turks, both of them. Nationalism has made them go out of Islam. Islam gathers, while nationalism parcels and separates. Yes.

Therefore, now, first the Islamic world is not going to find a way. They are still asking for salvation, to bring a solution for their problems through Western rules. It is impossible! An axe is just coming on all Arabs, all Muslim countries.

---

[139]Corruption, depravity, wickedness, immorality.

[140]*"If you [believers] support Allah, He will support you."* (47:7)

[141]The divinely-appointed leader whose coming at the End-Time of this world prior to the second coming of Jesus is mentioned in numerous *ahadith*.

And also for the global problems of this world, if people do not come to Islam, they are never going to find solutions, whether Germans, English, French, Italians, Americans, Chinese, Japanese. They have money but they haven't any solution for their problems. And they understand now that it is not enough only to have a thousand tons of gold reserves or to change their monies into another name, euros or pounds or dollars. They may have trillions, but trillions of dollars can't bring a solution to their problems.

They must understand! Now they are finished. Impossible, till they say, "O our Lord, You are our Lord. We are asking to follow Your rules." If not, they should be ground up, they should be taken away, and *dunya* should be cleaned.

May Allah forgive us and send us, from His powers, authorized lions, who, if you look at them, your heart will tremble, your feet can't stand up. I am asking from the Lord of Heavens to send them to us, to show those foolish people what is the power of *iman*,[142] what is the power of believing in Allah Almighty, what is the honour and power of those who are servants of the Lord of Heavens—to tremble, to come and say, "You must be our rulers, according the rules of our Lord."

No way now for all the world. Globally; it is closed down, locked. May Allah forgive us and send us Mehdi ﷺ! *Fateha*, for the honour of the most honoured one!

---

[142]Faith.

Heh! I was asking to speak to our Turkish people in Turkish. This is for Arabs and all the world's people—for the whole world.

I am here, *insha'allah;* I am here. What I am saying is the truth; *this is the truth.* And we are asking for a truth defender and we are asking for true ones to be sent, to take the reins of everything on earth. Otherwise, people are rubbish now; those who do not use heavenly rules; they are rubbish in the Divine Presence. No value for them. They should be carried to the dustbin.

Beware, O people! You must understand. And ask from Allah Almighty to send us quickly His lions. When lions come, jackals quickly run away.

Bismillahi-r-Rahmani-r-Raheem. If they do not believe, I am here, looking at them, what they can do.

Oh, U.N., U.N., United Nations! [Chuckles.] Each day Shaytan is coming, and they are making Shaytan the chairman in the U.N. His title is "Doctor Shaytan, Ph.D." [laughter], the Chairman of U.N., sitting.

Others are sitting down. They are not looking and seeing him, sitting above them and saying, "I am the Chairman, the real Chairman, not An-am Man-am.[143] No; I am here! What I say in his ear, he must say, he *must* say. He can't say anything else!"

---

[143] A play on the name of Kofi Annan, who was the Secretary-General of the United Nations at the time of this talk.

May Allah forgive us and bless you! You understand, Pakistani people? Pakistani people, 125 million. And Bangladesh is also 150 million, and they used a lady to be *imam*,[144] *masha'Allah!* For so many years they were 'praying' behind a lady.[145] [Laughter.]

Pakistan, also—Benazir, a lady. "It is good to get up and make a *khutbah*."[146] [Laughter.] How many *'ulama* do they claim, while putting Benazir to be their *imam* and she was ruling them? A woman can't be the *imam* of a *masjid*.[147] Then how can she be *imam* for 125 million Pakistani people?

Then they were fed-up with her and brought a soldier. Because their *'ulama*, half of them, are in love with money, from wherever money comes, it is all right. Some of them are also heedless; they do not know what they are doing, what should be. And Indian Muslims are in another situation, everywhere. There are 150 millions Muslims in India, but many of them are either ignorant or heedless people. Like a flock, whereever shepherds send them, they go. *Allah Allah Allah! Fateha.*[148]

---

[144]Leader; specifically, the leader of a congregational prayer.

[145]A subtle comment on the fact that, although women may not lead a congregational prayer in which men are present, both Bangladesh and Pakistan, preominantly Muslim nations, have been ruled by female heads-of-state.

[146]Sermon.

[147]Mosque.

[148]For the honor of [surat-] al-Fateha.

17

"O MANKIND, YOU HAVE BEEN HONOURED!"

A'udhu bil-Lahi min ash-Shaytani-r-rajim. Bismillahi-r-Rahmani-r-Raheem.

As He likes. We are living under His Mercy Oceans. We are humble servants to the Lord of Heavens, the Lord of Adam, the Lord of Abraham, the Lord of Moses, the Lord of Jesus Christ, the Lord of Muhammad, peace be upon them, and the Lord of all prophets and saints and all creation.

We are created to be His servants, and the Lord of mankind who created us and honoured us to be His deputies on earth, He is asking from us, from the children of Adam, to be His loyal servants.

He, Almighty, honoured them to be His honourable servants, not ordinary servants, and those who are His servants, no doubt they are honourable servants, not ordinary ones. Servanthood to the Lord of Heavens, that is the highest servanthood for everyone, and every creature wants to reach that most honoured servanthood. But that highest honour of being servants to the Lord of Heavens is granted only to the children of Adam.

Angels are honourable servants, but their levels are different from the levels of the Children of Adam. We are believers in holy books and in all the prophets who have been sent by Heavens. Some of them we may know and some others we do not know, also. And we have been ordered by the Lord of Heavens to believe in Him, in His existence, in His dominions, and no one can imagine the greatness of His Dominion Oceans. Everything that is in existence, beside the Lord's Dominion Oceans, is nothing.

You may imagine there to be a universe millions and trillions of times [bigger], but it is going to be only a very small point. It is not a real thing because real existence is only for Allah. Everything is in His magnificent and glorious Dominion Oceans. No one can imagine His greatness—impossible! As much as you may think about His Greatness, our imagination is only imagination, and imagination is not Reality. Therefore, mankind will always remains at their imagination level. What they are imagining about His Greatness is only imagination; it is not Reality.

Therefore, we have been honoured to know about His existence and to believe in His Unity, in His Oneness, in His unlimited Power Oceans and unlimited Dominion Oceans. No one can think about it or imagine it! As we said, everything that we know about Him is according to our imagination power, and imagination is never going to be real existence.

He is the Creator. He is the Creator and we are creatures. As much as He grants to us, even through our imagination, it is enough for us to be happy, to be lighted, to be honoured, to be glorious in His divine servanthood, so that the highest honour is granted to those who accept His servanthood.

Each prophet and each messenger who came called people to accept that honourable servanthood to their Lord. The entire world is nothing, and all prophets warned mankind not to be cheated by the tricks of Shaytan. If anyone accepts prophets' invitation to their Lord, the Lord of Heavens promises them to be with His endless dominions for eternity, for eternal honour in thee eternal life. Therefore, to be Muslim means surrendering and accepting the honourable servanthood to the Lord of Heavens, whose Names are countless. And we know that His most honoured Name is 'Allah'.

We are asking from Allah to be as He likes—as we said, to accept to be His servants, honoured servants. But Shaytan is cheating people and taking them away from His servanthood to the dirtiest slavery to this life. For a very short time [of temporary freedom and enjoyment], people are losing that endless honour and honourable servanthood to the Divine Presence.

I am sorry to say that people now are not looking at the real mission of all the prophets. They think that the Last Message coming from Heavens is different from others. No! It is a continuous message from the beginning, from Adam up to the end, up to Sayyidina Muhammad, peace be upon him and upon them. But they think that the mission of the Seal of the Prophets, Sayyidina Muhammad ﷺ, was another mission.

No. Adam called people, his children, to Allah. And then Noah called people to their Lord, to Allah, but they escaped. Abraham, also, he called people to their Lord, to their Lord's honourable servanthood, but they refused. And

Moses called Pharaoh and his nation to accept the most honoured and honourable servanthood, but they escaped. Jesus Christ's mission was also to call people to his Lord and to their Lord's most honoured and honourable servanthood,[149] but they escaped and wanted to kill him, and his Lord saved him.[150] And Sayyidina Muhammed, the Seal of Prophets, was on the same line, no difference.

I am speaking to those people who have never heard about the mission of Sayyidina Muhammad ﷺ. Therefore, I am making clear for everyone that each prophet's mission was to call people to the most honoured and honourable servanthood in their Lord's Divine Presence, and to be granted eternal life, eternal honour, eternal light forever. Therefore I am, as a humble servant, calling now to all the world's people, who are fighting among themselves for nothing.

Nations are making wars for nothing, and true religion, the mission of prophets, never accepted wars or fighting. Even if it is necessary, wars are only against devils, against Shaytan, whom they are opposing—the most terrible and dangerous enemies of the children of Adam, who want to cheat them, to keep them from reaching that endless honour, wanting people to be thrown into Hells as *they* are going to be thrown.

Therefore, now I am sorry to say that people, like Christians, Jews, even Muslims, are forgetting the real mis-

---

[149]*"Indeed, Allah is my Lord and your Lord, so worship Him. This is a straight path."* (3:51, 19:36, 43:64) These and numerous other verses make it clear that Jesus was a prophet like others, who never claimed divinity for himself.

[150]3:54-55; 4:157-158, 5:117/120 in Yusuf Ali's translation.

sion of their prophets and fighting each other. We are not happy with them; the Lord of Heavens is also not happy with them. The Lord of Heavens is saying, "O mankind, to be in peace is the greatest honour,[151] here and Hereafter. Keep peace among yourselves. Don't call for *dunya*, for this world, because this world and everything on it or under is not for anyone."

Everyone leaves it and goes. Don't quarrel, don't fight other nations and one another because it is foolishness. It is not going to be for anyone. You must try to reach the pleasure of your Lord. That is the whole mission of prophets.

Thank you for attending , for your attention to these few words. We may speak about it for hours and days, but it is enough. If we give a small message to all people, we are thankful to our Lord, Almighty Allah. *As-salamu 'alaikum,*[152] greetings to every believer! Thank you.

---

[151] "*As-sulh khair*, peace/reconciliation is best." (4:128)
[152] "Peace be upon you," the Islamic greeting.

18

THE OTTOMAN ISLAMIC LEGACY

Yaumun mubarak![153] It is a holy day in the holy month, Muharram, Muharram ul-Haram.[154] Today is the ninth of Muharram, tomorrow the tenth. May Allah open from His endless Mercy Oceans and endless Blessing Oceans for His most beloved servant's *ummah*,[155] *ummata Muhammad* ﷺ.

May Allah forgive us and send His heavenly support for His weak servants. The weakest servants, as we are seeing, are Muslims. Everywhere, unbelievers; everywhere, atheist people; everywhere, satanic trips and traps are filling East and West. And Muslims are bewildered, confused about what they can do because there is no help for them.

---

[153] A blessed day.

[154] Holy Muharram, the first month of the Islamic calendar. The tenth of Muharram is especially sacred for Muslims.

[155] Faith community, nation.

Since eighty years, no help for Islam—finished! It is recorded that on this day, the last *khalifa's Jum'ah*[156] ceremony took place in Asithane in Istanbul in 1924. This day was the last Friday ceremony, that had continued for six hundred years—finished. And look what was the situation when they left the Ottomans' way and said, "We are Turks"[157] — what happened to them, going up or going down? Since eighty years, they have never gone up but have gone down.

And the Islamic world, also, when the *Jöntürks* threw out the caliph of the Islamic world, no Islamic country—not even Hijaz or Egypt or Damascus or Baghdad or India or any other Islamic country—welcomed the last *khalifa*, and he was obliged to go to Europe as a *multaji*, refugee, going and waiting for them to help him and support him.

When the caliph passed away, he was *madyun*.[158] He had taken a loan from someone in Europe and he wasn't able to pay back his debt; and that person said, "I will hold the caliph's body till you pay his debt." So they fell down, those Turks, Young Turks. And someone collected and gave back that debt and took his body, and he is buried in

---

[156]Friday, the day of obligatory congregational worship in Islam. The last sultan-caliph was Abdel-Mecid???.

[157]For centuries, the Ottoman Empire had been the home, and even a haven, for people of many different ethnicities and religions, whose rights were honoured and guaranteed by the Islamic *Shari'ah*. But when the Empire was abolished and the nation of Turkey (Türkiye) established, the nation, its policies and national interests replaced God as the ultimate source of authority and object of loyalty.

[158]In debt.

Damascus in the mosque of Sultan Selim,[159] the caliph's ancestor who had conquered Damascus and Egypt.

Six hundred years earlier, Sultan Selim had reached Cairo. And he had with him the *Shareef*[160] of Makkatu-l-Mukarramah,[161] who brought the holy keys of the Holy Ka'bah and gave them to the *sultan*. And the *Shareef* said, "You are now the *hakim*[162] of the holy land."

But when the *khatib* gave the *khutbah*[163] in front of Sultan Selim and said, "Hakim al-Haramayn ash-Shareefayn,"[164] Sultan Selim said, "No!" And the Sultan stood up and said, "Correct your *khutbah*. Don't say 'Hakim!' *Al-Hakim huwa Allah.*'[165] Instead, say, 'The servant of the two holy mosques.' Then I will accept."

Sultan Selim was granted the holy *amanat*[166] from Makkatu-l-Mukarramah that belonged to Rasul-Allah ﷺ—his flag, his sword, his turban and his clothes, several holy things. They were brought to Istanbul and put as *amanat*

---

[159] Yavuz Sultan Selim (1465-1520) was the first Ottoman caliph, who extended Ottoman rule to Mecca and Medina

[160] The governor of Hijaz and its two holy mosques *(al-Haramayn ash-Shareefayn)*, Masjid al-Haram in Mecca and the Prophet's Mosque in Medina.

[161] Mecca the Honoured.

[162] Ruler.

[163] *Khatib:* prayer leader; *khutbah*: sermon.

[164] Ruler of the two sacred mosques.

[165] "Don't say 'Ruler. The Ruler is Allah,"

[166] Trust; that is, the sacred relics of the Prophet ﷺ, which are kept in Topkapı Museum in Istanbul.

muqaddisah.¹⁶⁷ And when those holy things that had been kept in Makkatu-l-Mukarramah were brought, the *sultans* [in Istanbul] looked after those holy things. And the *sultans* appointed twenty-four *qaris*.¹⁶⁸ For six hundred years, night and day in that place, each one sat and recited the Holy Qur'an for one hour, not stopping it for six hundred years. Then those *Jöntürks* came and it finished.

Therefore, now, Muslims are repenting. But our ancestors did this. They took the wrong way, wrong way. To follow Western countries is the wrong way. No; we have everything, we have been granted everything. We are not in need to follow Western people.

What happened when we followed Western people? We left everything that belonged to our culture, the Islamic *turath*, heritage. And everything we left, they are taking. They are saying, "Westernized Muslims." Western countries are in *kufr* and we are Muslims. How are we putting *kufr* with *iman*?¹⁶⁹ Can't!

[Shaykh Nazim addresses converts:] You are Muslim now. Do you now accept the culture you had before Islam, that you grew up in, keeping it? No. You left it and came to Islamic culture. But our foolish leaders who are destroying Islam and *ghafil*, heedless, Muslims are saying, "We must be like the West."

---

¹⁶⁷A sacred trust.
¹⁶⁸Reciters of the Qur'an.
¹⁶⁹Unbelief with faith?

Say, "We are not Muslim"—finished! Why are you carrying Islam with you? No! Change your name because you have changed everything else in your life, finished. No not leaving Islam and saying, "We are Western people, like Western people." No, can't be!

Therefore I am saying that the weakest people are Muslims, who want to be free to keep their Lord's commands, heavenly orders, but they are not given a chance, also. And I am asking from Allah Almighty, who always helps during this holy month, Muharram.

On the tenth of Muharram, Adam ﷺ landed on earth from Paradise and Allah Almighty accepted his *taubah*, repentance, and forgave him. And on that day, Noah ﷺ was saved from the Flood; Ibrahim ﷺ was saved from fire of Nimrod; Sulaiman ﷺ was granted his *sultanat*; Moses ﷺ was saved from Pharaoh and passed through the sea; and Yunus, Jonah, ﷺ got out of the *hut*, whale. Each prophet was granted something on the day that is coming tomorrow, the tenth of Muharram. Divine power came to all the prophets and heavenly support came for Muslims. Therefore I am asking, "O our Lord, grant us a little bit of that support in order that we may lift up our heads."

We are not walking on earth only like this [heads down]. Everywhere they are accusing us. If they look and see a Muslim, they accuse him, saying, "That is a fundamentalist, that is a terrorist."

May Allah take them away and clean the world from satanic people, from devils and from evil! That is our only prayer, nothing else; nothing else. This only must be your goal. It is not a goal to reach the imitation titles of this life.

Finally, everything is going to be nothing. Millions of people are under our feet. They are buried in cemeteries in so many places that are now fields, gardens, jungles or buildings—finished!

A person's relative died and he was so sorry. And in his heart he asked Bahlul Dana—Bahlul Dana, a beloved one, a friend of the Prophet ﷺ—for the love of Allah Almighty and His Prophet and His friends, not for any love of this life, this dirty life, saying, "O Bahlul, I am burying my beloved one now. I am putting a stone. What do you think should be written on it?"

And Bahlul, that servant of Allah Almighty, laughed and said, "Oh! Write on it, 'I am that one who yesterday was walking on grass, and now grass is growing on me.'" Understand? "Yesterday I stepping on green grass but today green grass is growing on me."

O people, *awliyas'* words are so sweet and full of wisdoms. *That* should be; *that* should be, finally. Therefore, take more care of servanthood. Put servanthood first. Fulfill it. Then see what is written for you to do for getting *halal rizq*, lawful provision.

Don't do anything at nighttime. Those people must leave nighttime activities. Nighttime, after *'Isha*,[170] the whole world must be in darkness, people asleep. As long as people are living night life, finished. They are just in the

---

[170] The fifth prayer of the day, observed at night.

hands of devils. No peace for them, no happiness for them, here or under the earth or on the Day of Resurrection.

O people, we are calling you to the right way. Leave the wrong way! Those whom you see that are outside at nighttime are on the wrong way and they are followers of Shaytan.

May Allah forgive me! Perhaps now for fifteen days—no, no; perhaps for one month—I have not been able to address you, but during this holy month, our Grandshaykh is granting me a little bit of power to address you about what you are in need of. And you must try to ask for something that belongs to your eternal life. Don't waste your time with such things that are going to finish today or tomorrow. Death is waiting for everyone. We don't know when it will reach us, but we must try to reach Allah and He is happy with us.

May Allah forgive us! For the honour of the most honoured one in His Divine Presence, Sayyidina Muhammad ﷺ—*Fateha!* ▲

19

KNOWING YOURSELF

A'udhu bil-Lahi min ash-Shaytani-r-rajeem. Bismillahi-r-Rahmani-r-Raheem.

For a long time I have not come here, and I am in need of a rest. Today our South African brothers and sisters are coming, and respected Professsor D'Costa is coming from the end of Africa, its farthest point.

Bismillahi-r-Rahmani-r-Raheem. Our *imam*, who is the most important pillar in the Most Distinguished Naqshbandi Order, Shaykh Bahauddin Naqshbandi, was saying that our *tariqah* is just built on association with the shaykh. And if the shaykh is not ready to speak to people, those who have been authorized by the shaykh to speak, to make Association with people, that must be, even for a short time. If you can find the time in which you can milk two sheep (that may take five minutes), you must not leave off Association.

If two brothers or sisters come together and they aren't able to do anything else, one of them may say, "*Ashhadu an la ilaha illa-Llah,"*[171] and the second may say, *"Wa ana ashhadu anna Muhammadan 'abduhu was rasulihu, salla-Lahu 'alayhi wa salam."*[172]

Ya Rabb,[173] keep us on this true belief, so that, whoever keeps this, he may open his entrance to Paradise. No one can enter Paradise without using that key, the key of Heavens, the key of Paradises. What is that? *"La ilaha illa-Llah, Muhammdan Rasul-Allah,"*[174] and to say, "I am witnessing to the *mawjudiyat*, existence, and the Oneness of Allah Almighty who created everything and gives all things what they need."

Nothing can be hidden from Allah Almighty—impossible, because He created everything. If He created, how is He not going to know? Nothing can be in existence if Allah Almighty does not put it in existence. Therefore, you may say, "Oh-ho! This atmosphere is full of atoms. Yes, we are breathing. How can He know what is coming in and what is going out?"

He *must* know, *must* know. Can't be hidden! If it is hidden, it means it has not come into existence. Don't use your balance for Allah; no.[175] He is the Creator, He is the Lord of everyone, of everything in existence. And every-

---

[171] "I bear witness that there is no deity except Allah."

[172] "And I bear witness that Muhammad is His slave and His messenger, peace and blessings be on him."

[173] O Lord.

[174] "There is no deity except Allah, Muhammad is the messenger of Allah."

[175] That is, an infinitesimal, human-sized scale of measurement or evaluation.

thing is saying, "O my Lord, glory be to You!" Everything glorifies Allah, and He knows, *subhanallah!* Don't use you measure to understand Allah Almighty. No, leave Him. You can't understand the real being of an *ant*. Leave it!

Do you know yourself, who you are? You may say, "I am Shaykh Hasan."

"From where?"

"From Germany."

That is your identity, yes? You know nothing else about yourself? Who are you? You are different from that one, and he is different from *that* one. Everyone has a special situation, special foundation, special identity. You are one. There can't be another one like you.

Who are you? How did you come? How do you live? How will you leave this life? From where did you come? Do you think that you came from the womb of your mother? How did you enter in it, how did you come out? Who are you?

Today you are here. Tomorrow someone else will come, you will disappear. A hundred years ago, no one here was in existence. Now we are in existence. Tomorrow—that means in the coming fifty or sixty or one hundred years—none of us is going to be.

How did it happen? So many millions of people, they lived in the same area. Where are they? They have become imagination, no reality. But there must be *something* of Reality that comes, lives here, and leaves this life and goes away.

There must be something in that imagination, there must be one point that belongs to Reality. What is that?

Men, in the twenty-first century, they do not leave the way of heedless people, letting themselves do as they like and going in nature or in space, and spending huge amounts of money and energy and effort. They want to go into space, making such instruments, rockets. They are saying, "We are going to go, to reach to a comet."

"Which comet?"

"Any comet. Eh! We want to reach there."

"Will you reach with your eyes?"

"No. We have put some instruments to look on our behalf."

"Your eyes are much more important than that instrument's looking. What is it that you want?"

They are saying, "We are trying to know the beginning of space, the beginning of our earth."

Such foolish people! What are you going to know? And everything has been sent from Heavens. Why are you not looking in the messages that the Creator of space and the universe sent to you, to look and to learn? What are you going to say?

They are saying [parodies:] "The Big Bang theory is just getting old and getting to be out of date, going to be useless. We must try to occupy the minds of people with another theory." They are saying, "Oh, we looked at those comets that make up such planets. They go everywhere and they make up new-born worlds' planets."

What happened? Are you riding on a comet to take these new planets for yourself, registering them for the Americans or the Russians? The Americans' rockets are going straight, Russians' going like this and coming on them. Therefore, the Russians are very unhappy. "Why this?" And after a while, the Americans' rockets are also going to disappear.

Look at yourself; ask about yourself! Why are you occupying yourself with nonsensical things? "Who are you?" I am asking, "and what is your mission? Do you know it now, after sending those rockets up?" No. Look at yourself, to learn your identity and your mission. But people are working for Shaytan!

Professor D'Costa: Almost a hundred per cent of people are working for Shaytan now. Perhaps among one million, you may find ten or you may find one hundred, but others are all working for Shaytan. That is the source of troubles on earth, because Shaytan is trying to give trouble. And the first trouble-maker was Shaytan.

When Allah Almighty ordered him to make *sajdah* to Adam and he refused, he caused the first trouble in the heavenly existence, making angels and every creature there unhappy because he made trouble. And he is continuing up to today, and he is going to make that trouble up to the end of this life.

Therefore, every trouble comes from Shaytan. Every trouble that people are falling into, unsolved problems, are from Shaytan, Shaytan's teaching. And as long as people are working for Shaytan, they are not going to reach peace on earth till the earth is destroyed with those people. As Allah destroyed the nation of Noah through the Flood, He is going to destroy all of Shaytan's workers. When they are destroyed, our planet is going to be clean.

"When it is clean" means that the people on earth will work for Allah because our oath on the Day of Promises was, "O our Lord, we are going to work for Your servanthood. We are not going to work for anyone else. That is our oath."[176] Now, everyone is forgetting that, and they are changing and saying, "We are working for Shaytan." May Allah forgive us!

O people, try to save yourself from the hands of devils, who are all representatives of Shaytan. Leave them; don't give them any support. If you give your support, you will fall into sufferings and miseries.

Come to the friends of Allah.[177] Try to be with them, to save yourself, to be clean, and try to clean from East to West, from North to South. Allah Almighty is promising whoever tries to do this, "I am is his supporter." Don't worry that you are only a handful of people. Doesn't matter! If Allah is with you, you are victorious.

The Titanic, *ma maghloub*,[178] was never going to be defeated; always a winner. Those who are with Allah are always winners and victorious. We are asking humbly from our Lord, Almighty Allah, for the honour of the most hon-

---

[176]Referring to 7:172. See footnote .

[177]*Awliya*.

[178]Not defeated, vanquished, beaten.

oured one in His Divine Presence, Sayyidina Muhammad ﷺ. *Fateha!* ▲

20

KEEPING ISLAMIC ORDERS

A'udhu bil-Lahi min ash-Shaytani-r-rajeem. Bismillahi-r-Rahmani-r-Raheem. La hawla wa la quwwata illa bil-Lahi-l-'Aliyi-l-'Azheem.

As-salamu 'alaykum! [*Mureeds* respond.] When *salam* stopped, troubles came.[179] Islam came with its perfection, and every command is a way to perfection. Commands are for doing something or for leaving off something. Every command makes a way to perfection.

From the outside, it appears that servanthood is for our Lord. But really, the benefit of servanthood is for ourselves because Allah Almighty is not in need of any benefit. When He creates, He does not ask for any benefit from His creatures. Creatures expect from Him; He does not expect anything. If anyone glorifies Allah Almighty, He is in any case glorified from eternity to eternity; glory is among His divine *siffat,* attributes. All creatures' glorifying is only such a small dot in His Glory Oceans.

---

[179]That is, due to anti-Islamic propaganda, the Islamic greeting, ordered by Allah, has fallen into disuse among many Muslims as being backward, antiquated and foreign.

Everything that you do is within limits, but what is with Him is unlimited. You may imagine all creatures' glorifying as bigger, bigger, bigger, bigger. But even if you imagine that spot to be ten times bigger, a hundred times bigger, a thousand times bigger, millions, trillions, quadrillions of times bigger, bigger, bigger, what is in it is this spot is within limits. But around it there are unlimited oceans.

Therefore, every command that orders you, "Do this," try to keep it. Don't be lazy! Don't follow your ego because *atalet*, laziness, is the unchangeable characteristic of our egos—*unchangeable!*

Our ego wants to eat and to sleep. Always, [parodies], "Give to me to eat and cover me to sleep"—the new *madhhab*,[180] new *tariqah* of egos that our youngsters are growing up with, the new generation's new lifestyle that they like. "Oh! No work, but give us something to eat and drink. Then put something on me to sleep." And third [Mawlana claps in rhythm], music, music.

Shaytan is asking for himself, "You, our Lord, You, the Lord of the Heavens—You have given to Your prophets, sending them holy books, and they are singing with Your holy books. I am asking for myself, also, for my followers, to be happy with *me*."

And the Lord of Heavens is saying, "I have just given you all the singers, musical people, who are making egos awaken, to get up and play, to dance and . . . [laughter].

Yes, everywhere! Look at that 'Shaytan-box'! For twenty-four hours young people are jumping, playing,

---

[180]School of thought or jurisprudence.

dancing, and those horns and drums are making Shaytan very happy, the Lord of Heavens saying, "All for you!" This is the new life-style that makes Shaytan very happy, getting the majority of people to follow him in such a way.

Those who are happy in such a way, they should be underground, and for their following shaytanic singing and playing, finally their tears are going to be blood and their teeth are going to be *jamr*, fire, *na'udhu bil-Lah!*[181]

Atalet! *Nafs*, ego, never wants get up, only because laziness it is its real characteristic, real characteristic. And now that bad characteristic is finding a very suitable atmosphere for itself everywhere.

People are free. They like to be, more lazy, and they are waiting, without doing anything, for everything to come to them for eating, drinking and dressing. That is their new way. They are not going to carry anything of their responsibility.

Therefore, you are seeing, in every country, young people running in the streets and asking for more freedom (what is 'more freedom'?),or more money, more money, *yaumiya*,[182] a salary, saying, "It is very little. We want more!" They are asking only for their egos—to work for a short time and to be paid more. This is their idea: to work as short a time as possible but with a high, the highest salary. That is a trick of Shaytan's.

---

[181] We seek refuge in Allah.
[182] Daily wages.

All the world is running in the streets. They are saying, "We don't like this prime minister. Change him!" Running in another country, saying, "I don't like this president. Take him down!" In another country, "We must elect another one to give us more freedom and the highest salaries." And so many of Shaytan's representatives are saying, "Yes, I am that one. Come to me! I shall give you the highest salary and the shortest working time." And people are running after him. "Oh, this is the best one, that is the best one."

But that person, when sitting at his table after election, finds a book in front of him, saying, "Oh, please don't give what you promised to your electors. Don't give! If you give, you will make them happy. Then there should be peace in your country. It is not our way to make peace among people. What you promised, don't look after it! You continue like your *salaf*, predecessors. The one who was here before, he did the same thing. You must follow his way, not what you promised people—no!"

Then [chuckles], beginning after one day, one week, one month, they are waiting. When his promise is not fulfilled, then people are going to be very angry, saying, "Next election, we will take that one down and bring another one"—in such a way. That is the shaytanic way.

The democratic system is just built on incorrect, wrong principles; can't be changed. Shaytan is trying not to give people peace, not just in Cyprus. No, everywhere. Shaytan never wants peace to come to countries, to people. No, no! Don't believe it!

Therefore we are saying that every heavenly command is really for your benefit, bringing you to a peaceful area, to a peaceful life, to an enjoyable life, to a lighted life, to an excellent life standard; but people are not patient and they do not believe. That is their punishment. Every command brings you satisfaction, brings you lights, brings you peace. And also, everything from which the Lord of the Heavens prevents you, every forbidden thing, is contrary to your peaceful life. If you go into it, you will lose that peaceful atmosphere, personally and collectively.

O people, try to keep heavenly orders, either commands or prohibitions. You should find yourself in a Paradise–like atmosphere here. Nothing of this life's troubles can reach you. You will be on the safe side, and you will have saved yourself from Trouble Oceans and have been taken out of them. But people are getting troubles, endless sufferings, in Trouble and Suffering Oceans.

For the sake of the most beloved one in the Divine Presence, Sayyidina Muhammad ﷺ, keep his way and keep the way of Paradise. Those who are following the Paradise way never face anything that hurts them physically or spiritually; but those who leave the Paradise way and come to the satanic way, there is no moment when they should be free from facing bad things. Always they should encounter bad things; troubles, sufferings, problems, miseries. Everything that is going to be for Hells' people, they should find on that way.

Don't come and ask me. So many people are coming and complaining. I am asking, "On which way are you going? Do you pray?"

"No."

Finished! I do not ask anything else. Ask him! If he is not praying, don't say anything. You are on the wrong way and *you* must carry this! If you want to save yourself, come to the Paradise way and everything will be all right for you.

May Allah forgive us and send us, from His lions, heavenly lions, to take away jackals, wolves, bears and foxes, to take away dragons and devils, and to destroy the *sultanat* of Satan! For the honour of the most honoured one in His Divine Presence, Sayyidina Muhammad ﷺ—*Fateha!*

Keep it! This is enough for all nations, for all the children of Adam, not any other way. No one can say what we are saying now. It is the summary of all holy books. May Allah forgive me! ▲

21

SEEKING KNOWLEDGE THAT BENEFITS

A'udhu bil-Lahi min ash-Shaytani-r-rajeem. Bismillahi-r-Rahmani-r-Raheem. La huwla wa la quwwata illa bil-Lahi-l-'Aliyi-l-'Azheem.

It is an Association. Professor D'Costa: Who is a professor? He is that one who, if he is asked, may answer about everything. If not, he is not a professor. *Ya Allah, ya Allah! 'Alim, ya Rabbi! Subhanak! Subhanak!*[183]

'Ilm, knowledge—if Allah Almighty grants it to His servant, he may know. That is *'ilmu-n-nafiy'a*, knowledge that gives benefit. *'Ilm* must give benefit. It is not a *zeena*, decoration, ornament; no. *'Ilm*, knowledge, is a grant from Allah Almighty, to make a way to His Divine Presence. That is the real purpose of knowledge.

Why do we learn? For everything that you study and learn, what is your goal? Now people are learning only for *dunya*.[184] And you are in *dunya* but you are still asking for

---

[183] O Allah, O Allah! Teach, O my Lord! Glory be to You! Glory be to You!
[184] This world.

more *dunya*, much more. "If I have ten dollars today, tomorrow I must get a hundred. What is the way to reach a hundred dollars? I must see. I am trying to learn the way that I can get a thousand dollars."

Then Shaytan is saying, "No! You must try to reach ten thousand. See what is the way."

Everything, every knowledge that is not good knowledge, is from Shaytan. Shaytan is teaching people to reach more of *dunya*, and urging them and whipping them. As a rider whips horses, Shaytan whips people to reach more of *dunya*.

Therefore, the Prophet ﷺ was saying, "*Allahumma, innee as'aluka 'ilma-n-nafiy'an,*"[185] asking from Allah Almighty, "O my Lord I am asking from You real knowledge that make me closer to Your Divine Presence." And another prayer of Rasul-Allah ﷺ says, "*Allahumma, innee a'udhu bika min 'ilm la yanfa'.*[186] O my Lord I take refuge in You from learning that makes me run away from You, to run after *dunya*."

Where are our people now? All the world is listening to Allah, asking for Allah, or asking for *dunya*? "*Innahum la yuflihun.*"[187] If they continue on that way, they will never reach anything good for themselves here or Hereafter; they will lose everything that Allah Almighty is promising. He is promising His servants eternal life, but Shaytan is calling people to something that is only going to be imaginary.

---

[185] "*O Allah, indeed I ask You for beneficial knowledge.*" (Hadith)

[186] "*O Allah, indeed I seek refuge with You from knowledge that does not benefit.*" (Hadith)

[187] "*Indeed, they [the wrong-doers] will not be successful,*" a paraphrase of 28:37.

Now today, so many people here may be of different ages. They may be ten years old, twelve years, twenty, thirty, forty, fifty, sixty, seventy, eighty, ninety. What, so many years have passed? Now what remains with you of so many years? You are just living in this moment now, and after a while that will also be taken to a non-existent world. And non-existent means imagination.

You can make a fire and you can put so many things on the fire—of wood, of furniture; so many things you may put on it and leave. After one hour, come and see what remains there. Ashes. Yes, finished. Where is what you put on it? And now time is taking everything from you, burning, making ashes, and there is coming a storm and ashes. [Mawlana claps his hands to indicate "finished".]

And when the Lord of Heavens orders this globe, our planet, to explode from its center in space, after seconds you will not find even atoms because what keeps atoms in existence, in such order, is the command of Allah Almighty to keep atoms in their center. What is in the center? Protons and neutrons, and electrons orbiting around it. If Allah Almighty's order does not keep that system, the atom is going to disappear. Electrons will go away, and also protrons and neutrons.

And the whole world, also. By His order, each part is keeps the other. When His order comes, saying, "Leave! Go as you came. From wherever you came, return back," in seconds or less than seconds—thirds, fourths, fifths of a second—it is going to disappear. If He orders the universe, "Go back to your real position" from where it came into Power Oceans," it will go back and the universe will finish; nothing in space—finished, and space will remain in its original condition of deep darkness, with nothing in it. If

He orders, "As you came in existence before, come back," this space will become full of stars and galaxies and suns.

And space is only deep darkness. No one knows what space is—from where it begins, where it ends, and from where these things in it have come, because shaytanic teachings are preventing them to ask or learn or teach such things.

Everything that takes away from Allah Almighty is a shaytanic teaching. And people now have just fallen into it. No one is happy, no one is in peace now. There are exceptions but they are not common, and exceptions never change the general situation. Commonly, people are ignorant. They are not learning and they are following Shaytanic teachings, *'ilm la yanfa'*, which is learning that never gives benefit to its holders here and Hereafter.

Therefore, we are asking from Allah Almighty, "*Ya Rabbi*, let us reach something of Your grant that You granted to Your respected and honoured servants, Your messengers, particularly the Seal of the Prophets, Sayyidina Muhammad ﷺ. You granted him from real knowledge that brings men to perfection and makes them Your servants, preparing them for that perfection and for reaching their Lord's pleasure. We are asking for *that*."

And now it is just closed down and there are only satanic teachings around the world, making people to be more violent, to be farther away from their real being, making them run away from what they have been created for, the ones created as servants to Allah Almighty's Divine Presence. We have been honoured to be servants and to be granted servanthood to His Divine Presence, but people are not learning servanthood to their Creator, to their Lord. They are running to learn satanic knowledge, and they are respecting and worshipping Shaytan.

When Allah Almighty sent Prophet Noah ﷺ to his nation, calling his people to Allah, to their Lord, to their Creator, they ran away, not accepting. They said, "We know our way. Our teachings are just the opposite of yours. We are happy with our teachings and we are not following you." And Allah Almighty sent the flood on them, and everywhere, from every step of the earth, fountains came, and from above, also, rain came. And the flood came and took everything away.

Now it is same, but in another way. Now, everywhere you go, there is a fountain of troubles and problems—everywhere! Look, the whole world is full! At every step you should find a problem, a trouble. People have just been graduated by Shaytan to be trouble-makers. Men, women, old ones, young ones, learned ones, ignorant ones—all of them are trouble-makers, graduated.

Look at that 'Shaytan-box' to see how people are running in the streets, everywhere trouble, trouble! No one is at rest, no one is in peace; no one is hopeful, all of them are hopeless. They are drowning in Trouble Oceans because everyone is making trouble. No one is holding himself back from trouble. Everyone is becoming a trouble-maker, pouring his troubles on mankind. And people are just drowning, from East to West, from North to South, in those Trouble Oceans and problems, miseries and sufferings. No one is exempt.

Therefore, people are running to be drunk, to forget these troubles. So many kinds of alcohol and so many kinds of drugs they are using. For what? To forget, not to feel their troubles, as a doctor gives drugs to a patient with too much pain. But it is not a *tedavi*, cure. It is not a cure, only given as a painkiller, not taking away the sickness or illness. Now people are running to drugs, running at least to smoke, and alcohol is everywhere. For what? Not to feel the pain. Everything is a painkiller!

O people, come to the true way! Come and ask from true ones. Don't think that true ones have finished, no. True ones are never going to finish, but they are hidden, hiding themselves. They are hidden, but if you ask, if you look carefully, you can find one in East or West. If not asking, you can't find one because everyone coming in front of you is a representative of Shaytan.

Therefore, the Prophet ﷺ was saying, *'Utlubu-l-'ilm wa law fis-Seen.*[188] O people, you should ask, for real knowledge that saves you from troubles, from devils here, and from Hells on the Last Day. To learn that knowledge, if you can find it at that farthest distance (at that time China was the farthest country), you must run to learn."

And knowledge is not from books, showing that, if it were through books, the Prophet ﷺ would have said to bring that knowledge from China in books and learn here. Rather, he is indcating that you must go to the one who has such knowledge.

---

[188]*"Seek knowledge even if [it be] in China."* (Hadith)

A person is teaching you, not a book teaching you. You can take knowledge from those people whose hearts are full of that knowledge. Don't think that you can read books and learn, no. Therefore, *"Wa law fis-Seen"* indicates that if the one who has that knowledge is in China, you must go to him, to learn from him. But now Wahhabi people are saying, "No, no need. You can read books, you can learn by yourself."

O people, come to the true way and ask for true ones if you would like to be happy and in peace here and Hereafter, and make your Lord, Almighty Allah, pleased with you. If not, everyone is just buried in his grave, and no one can help another one in his grave.

May Allah forgive me and bless you! I am saying this to all mankind, and it is knowledge that is from the four holy books, particularly from the Holy Qur'an, coming through the most beloved servant of Allah Almighty, the most honoured one, to whom the Last Message, the Holy Qur'an, was sent—to be servants of that one and to ask knowledge from him and from his successors, the successors of the Prophet ﷺ. *Bi-hurmati-l-Fateha.*[189] ▲

---

[189] For the honour of *al-Fateha* [the opening *surah* (chapter) of the Qur'an].

22

THE NECESSITY OF BELIEVING IN THE LAST MESSENGER

A'udhu bil-Lahi min ash-Shaytani-r-rajeem. Bismillahi-r-Rahmani-r-Raheem. La hawla wa la quwwata illa bil-Lahi-l-'Aliyi-l-'Azheem.

Traditional knowledge, which is real knowledge coming from Heavens as revelations, reached the earth and the hearts of people. If finding hearts open, it entered. If they were closed, locked, it couldn't.

Therefore, Allah Almighty sent the Prophet, the Seal of Prophets, Sayyidina Muhammad ﷺ, with His last message, the last of the holy books, *Qur'an al-Kareem*, the Holy Qur'an. Those whose hearts were open heard and listened and obeyed. They were the believers who believed in Allah Almighty and, through His messengers, particularly the Seal of the Prophets, their hearts were opened.

At the time of Sayyidina Muhammad ﷺ, in the land where he lived, there were Jewish people as well as neighbouring Christians, the Book-Given People.[190] They had been granted holy books through their prophets, and they claimed that they believed in Allah Almighty and believed in His messages as holy books coming from Heavens, and they also claimed that Allah Almighty had sent some special beings from among His servants as prophets. They believed; they were not like idol worshippers, no.

And they knew what had happened in past times during the historical periods that were mentioned in their holy books—the beginning of creation, and the creation of Adam and Eve, may Allah bless them. They believed, and through their beliefs they knew that after Sayyidina Adam ﷺ, Allah Almighty had sent prophets, one after another.

They had that knowledge. But when the Seal of the Prophets ﷺ came with his holy book, the Holy Qur'an, they first came against his prophethood and they were among the first deniers of his holy book, the Holy Qur'an.

It is the biggest blame on Keepers of the Book to do that. Up to today, they are carrying that blame. Still they are not saying that the Seal of Prophets, Sayyidina Muhammad ﷺ, was sent as the last prophet up to end of the world. That is the biggest blame on them and they should be punished.

They are saying that Mars is a planet. And they are looking at the moon, saying, "No, we do not accept this moon. We only accept Mars." Two thousand or four thou-

---

[190] *Ahl al-Kitab*, People of the Scripture, Jews and Christians, the sister religions of Islam.

sand years ago, for Noah and Moses and Jesus Christ and Abraham, peace be upon them, you were saying, "Oh, prophets! They are stars in the sky of prophethood." And the moon, full moon, has come but you are saying, "No!" What is that foolishness?

Allah should ask them. Before the Last Day, they should be asked and they should be punished. It is the biggest blame, biggest sin, on them not to say that Sayyidina Muhammad ﷺ is a prophet who was sent with a holy book, the last holy book, the Holy Qur'an. And they are without shame, saying about the Seal of Prophets, Sayyidina Muhammad ﷺ, "Our hearts are locked and our ears do not hear what you are saying, and nothing enters our hearts of what you are reciting. We do not accept you!"[191]

Yahu, if they were idol worshippers, it wouldn't matter. Idol-worshippers weren't given a holy book, but you, as Christians and Jewish people who are reciting your holy book, the Torah and *Evangelos*, Gospel, how are you saying, "You are not a prophet"?

If he is not a prophet, how has his power reached throughout 1500 years? His power is working in the hearts of people, and now, five times a day among about two billion people, muezzins go up on minarets and say, *"Ashhadu an la ilaha illa-Llah, wa ashhadu anna Muhammadu-r Rasul-Allah."*

How did that happen? If that person, Muhammad, who was orphaned from his father and mother, and after forty years stood up amidst unknown deserts and said, "O people, now I have been sent as the Last Messenger to you

---

[191] 2:7, 16:108-109.

with last message of Heavens, and you must say, '*La ilaha illa-Lah*, only one God, who is Allah, and Muhammad ﷺ is His servant and His prophet'"—*how?* By what power?

He stood up, one, alone, and his tribe were such, such, such jealous, such ignorant people. When he said, "I have come to destroy your idols, and I have come to you to make you believe in one God, who is Allah, our Creator," there was not nothing in his hand except maybe a cane.

He said that. What could they do? What did they do to him? They tried to do everything to take him away and to extinguish the lights that he brought from Heavens, but they were not able to do that. They did their worst for him and for the believers, and finally they wanted to take his life, to kill him.

But he said, "I am under my Lord's protection. You can't do anything. But I am going, I am leaving." And he left his most beloved land, Mecca the Blessed, Makkatu-l-Mukarramah, and went away. For thirteen years [after the call to prophethood] he had been in Mecca, but finally, when they did their worst to him, he left for Madinatu-l-Munawwarah[192] emigrating from Mecca to Medina.

They went after him, they did not leave him alone. They thought that he was an ordinary person. "We can do everything to him," they were thinking. They went after him, fighting, fighting, fighting. Then they reached the limit of their enmity, finished, with no more power to go after him.

---

[192]Medina the Radiant.

Then Allah Almighty ordered, "Now you may go and conquer Makkatu-l-Mukarramah. O My beloved, most beloved servant, now prepare yourself to enter, to go back to your most beloved land. My House, the House of the Lord, *Bayt-Ullah*,[193] is there."

After eight years—yes, eight years—the Prophet ﷺ went and reached and conquered Makkatu-l-Mukarramah, the place of the House of the Lord. He broke every idol,[194] and Bilal[195] got up on the House of the Lord and said,

Allahu Akbar, Allahu Akbar, Allahu Akbar, Allahu Akbar.
Ashhadu an la ilaha illa-Llah, ashhadu an la ilaha illa-Llah.
Ashhadu anna Muhammadu-r-Rasul-Allah,
ashhadu anna Muhammadu-r-Rasul-Allah.
Hayya 'ala-s-salah, hayya 'ala-s-salah.
Hayya 'ala-l-falah, hayya 'ala-l-falah.
Allahu Akbar, Allahu Akbar.
La ilaha illa-Llah.[196]

---

[193] The Holy Ka'bah, also known as the Sacred House, the first place of worship of God, built in antiquity at Allah's command by the prophet Abraham with the help of his son, the prophet Ishmael.

[194] During the bloodless conquest of Mecca, the Prophet ﷺ toppled all the 360 idols that had been placed in the Sacred House by the Meccan pagans.

[195] The Prophet's muezzin, a former Abyssinian slave..

[196] The Call to Prayer *(adhan/ezan)*, which translates as:
    Allah is Most Great (four times).
    I bear witness that there is no deity except Allah (twice).
    I bear witness that Muhammad is the Messenger of Allah (twice).
    Come to prayer (twice).
    Come to salvation (twice).
    Allah is Most Great (twice).
    There is no deity except Allah.

As-salat wa-s-salam 'alayka, ya Rasul-Allah, haqqan wa sidqa.

As-salat wa-s-salam 'alayka, ya Nabi-Allah, haqqan wa sidqa.

As-salat wa-s-salam 'alayka, ya Habib-Allah, haqqan wa sidqa.[197]

Then what happened—*what happened?* They must look at the history of Islam not to speak ignorantly, no. But they are afraid to look at the history of Islam. They are afraid to look at the life of the Seal of Prophets. It is so, so magnificent!

And yet they are saying he was not a prophet. What is this? His name, that was granted to Adam through heavenly messages, is written in their scriptures,[198] and all prophets were saying his name and asking their nations to believe in him.[199] If they did not believe in him, their *iman*,

---

[197]The invocation of blessings on the Prophet, recited immediately following the Call to Prayer. Its meaning is:

Blessings and peace be on you, O Messenger of Allah, truly and sincerely.

Blessings and peace be on you, O Prophet of Allah, truly and sincerely.

Blessings and peace be on you, O beloved of Allah, truly and sincerely.

[198]This is mentioned in the following verse: *"And [mention] when Jesus son of Mary said, 'O Children of Israel, indeed I am the messenger of Allah to you, confirming what came before me of the Torah and bringing good tidings of a messenger to come after me whose name is Ahmed.'"* 'Ahmed' is another name of the Prophet, derived from the same three-letter root, H-M-D, as Muhammad, meaning "the Praised One.'"(61:6)

[199]Referring to the verse: *"And [recall, O people of the Scripture], when Allah took the covenant from the prophets, [saying], 'Whatever I give you of the Scripture and wisdom, and then there comes to you a messenger confirming what is with you, you must believe in him and support him.' He [Allah] said, 'Have you*

their faith, was of no value. If a person says, *"La ilaha illa-Llah,"* but does not say, *"Muhammadu-r-Rasul-Allah,"* his faith is unacceptable, of no value.

We are speaking about that knowledge that, if hearts are open, those lights will come, heavenly lights, and enter, given to those who open their hearts and accept. They are always fresh, they are always hopeful, they are always happy; they are always in peace, here and Hereafter.

May Allah forgive me and bless you! And I am calling all nations to look, one by one, to study the life of the Seal of the Prophets ﷺ before divine vengeance comes; to look at it once again, or divine vengeance will come and grind them, finishing. Allah's punishment is not only about *"Alam tara kayfa fa'ala Rabbuka bi-ashabi-l-feel?"*[200] those people who came from Yemen to destroy the House of the Lord, Allah Almighty saying, "Look what happened to them, O My beloved one, and look, all mankind, what I did to them, how I dealt with them.

---

acknowledged and accepted My covenant on that?' They said, 'We have acknowledged it.' He said, "Then bear witness, and I am with you among the witnesses.'" (3:81)

[200] *"Have you not considered, [O Muhammad,] how your Lord dealt with the People of the Elephant?"* (105:1). This *surah* reports what happened when Abraha, a powerful pagan king from Yemen, came to Mecca with his army, mounted on elephants, to attack and take over the Ka'bah. At the critical moment, Allah Almighty sent upon Abraha and his troops flocks of birds with pieces of hardened clay in their beaks and claws, which they dropped one by one on the invaders, who died of a deadly illness caused by the divinely-guided the missiles.

"When they came to destroy My House in Mecca, I sent birds on them, each one carrying three small pieces of clay, one in their beaks and two in their *pençe*, claws, and the birds threw those on them. Not one went wrong, coming right on target, *'Fa ja'alahum ka'asfin makoul,'*[201] making them like a field of wheat or barley that has been harvested up to the heads and nothing remains. I made them just like that harvested land, finishing."

Allah is looking now, but He is not sending such birds. He has left those unbelievers of today to make big flying birds with their hands —big birds, airplanes, aircraft, with bombs; to do everything as those birds did to those unbelievers, their nations preparing that huge power for each other, to make them like a land just harvested—finished!

O people, keep to the right path, keep with true ones. Then no harm will come to you. If you insist on the wrong way, the shaytanic way, you, that nation, is just going to be finished.

May Allah forgive me and bless you! I am asking forgiveness for all nations, to come and to say, *"La ilaha illa-Llah, Muhammadu-r-Rasul-Allah."* For the honour of the most honoured one in His Divine Presence, Sayyidina Muhammad ﷺ—*Fateha!* ▲

---

[201] *"And He made them like eaten chaff."* (105:5)

23

OPENING OUR HEARTS TO HEAVENLY LIGHTS THROUGH FAITH

A'udhu bil-Lahi min ash-Shaytani-r-rajeem. Bismillahi-r-A'udhu bil-Lahi min ash-Shaytani-r-rajeem. Bismillahi-r-Rahmani-r-Raheem. La hawla wa la quwwata illa bil-Lahi-l-'Aliyi-l-'Azheem.

Who is a fortunate one? A fortunate one is that one whose heart is opened and he is able to receive from heavenly inspirations.

Planes are not able to land everywhere. They need prepared areas to come and land on them. And from Heavens, angels aren't able to land on every heart. If it is an unprepared land, they aren't able to land on it, only on a heart if it is open. And the key for hearts, it is to say, *"La ilaha illa-Llah, Muhammadu-r-Rasul-Allah* ﷺ. I believe in God, Allah Almighty. I believe in His existence, and I believe in His Unity or Oneness." That opens hearts, preparing them. That person is going to be in connection with Heavens.

But no one can reach Heavens without a mediator. Not everyone can fly. If you want to fly from here to London, to

East or to West, you must use a plane. You must get in it and you may go, you may reach.

That is for our physical being, and our spirituality also can't reach Heavens and heavenly stations by itself. We must use mediators, who are prophets. Therefore, Allah Almighty sent prophets to every nation throughout the centuries from the beginning.

Sayyidina Adam ﷺ was the first one. Those who believed in him, that he brought heavenly orders and commands, those people who went with Adam were able to reach their heavenly stations. Those who did not accept remained on earth.[202]

And in such a way, reaching from the beginning to the end, thousands of prophets—124,000 prophets, according our traditional knowledge—came at different times, among different nations or communities. Prophets used their heavenly powers, and they took those who reached them, accepting, up to their heavenly stations.

Yes. When our hearts are open and we believe in all the prophets—and particularly in the last one, the Seal of the Prophets, Sayyidina Muhammad ﷺ, the most praised one, most beloved one, most respected one in the Divine Presence—then angels come and land on them, and give those people heavenly lights.

---

[202] According to traditional sources, a group of Adam's progeny remained faithful to the guidance that their grandfather, the first prophet, conveyed to them from Allah. Another group, the descendants of Cain, became corrupted, opposed their father, and made corruption on earth. Later, the Flood took them away.

Those lights coming into hearts reach every part of our bodies. Each cell takes its share. And when they take their shares, they change. They are not going to be only material parts, no; they are going to be like a lighted house in the darkness of night. If that light does not come into it, that house is going to be dark; when that light comes, it is lighted. And when angels come with those lights, those lights run through our veins, everywhere. Each cell takes its share, so that the fortunate one is that one whose whole physical being and cells are lighted. He is not in darkness; finished. And those who close their hearts, not opening them to accept what prophets brought so that there is no way for angels to come and enter their hearts, they are unfortunate people.

They are in darkness, and darkness gives people fear. They are fearful people and they are hopeless people. No hope for them for the coming days, and also no lights to make them be saved from fear. Those people who do not believe are always fearful because they are in darkness. When their hearts open and are lighted, they are fearless people. They will look and see; no fear for them.

Now people are in darkness; the twenty-first century's people are in darkness. Even though they may say, "Oh, through electricity the whole world is so bright and enjoyable and lighted at night time," that is imitation light. It shines outside, not shining in your heart.

Yes, everywhere, thousands and thousands, millions of lamps. What is the benefit? They are outside your heart. No benefit; never taking fear from your heart or giving you hope. And even though they are seeing millions, billions of lamps, if they look when the sun is rising, finished. Those lights are just finished, never giving anything to you, and people are looking for the sun to rise and shine.

Now people are not asking to reach faith and its lights that should be in their hearts, but they are enjoying themselves with their imitation lights. No! That is the source of the troubles and sufferings of people; otherwise this world is enough for everyone. Allah Almighty granted everything that mankind might need, but they are not happy and in satisfaction; no contentment for them. "We have everything, but no peace in our hearts. How can we be in peace?"

People are asking for peace, but if they do not accept, do not open their hearts to believe that lights come from Heavens, they will see those lights as coming from the sky. But the sun is not on earth, it is outside, in space. From there, from the sun, those lights are coming to the earth. How are you asking for lights from the earth? The earth is in darkness. And men, also, they are in darkness if they do not look and take lights from Heavens.

Those people who are taking heavenly lights, they are like suns. The sun gives its lights to material beings on earth, but those who are taking from Heavens' lights are reaching the real beings of mankind and saving them from darkness. They are going to reach safety and peace. According to their need, according to their efforts, according to their hearts, more openings, more lights are coming. In a small distance, a little bit comes; if fully opening, full heavenly lights are coming and entering.

Therefore, the Prophet ﷺ was saying, "There should come on my nation, when the Last Days approach, so many problems, and everyone going to fall into troubles because everyone is going to be a trouble-maker for himself and for others. Every place should be full of darkness and troubles, sufferings and miseries. But there should be *some* servants, not too many, among those people. They are going to be with them, living with them, but their position should be elevated. People are suffering, but at *their* station, spiritual station, there should be peace, absolute peace, not any trouble, no suffering. People are going to be in troubles, sufferings, but those people are not going to feel or to see sufferings or troubles. No problems for them because they are not trouble-makers."

All those who are trouble-makers must suffer, and suffering is a punishment for them—a punishment. Suffering is not a grant from Allah Almighty, no. Suffering is a punishment, and now people are under punishment. Communities, nations—nations within themselves and with other nations—all of them are in troubles. No rest, no comfort, no peace for them.

Therefore, O people, we are calling you to a lighted area. We are calling you to a safe way; we are calling you to a peaceful place. Come, don't run away! Whoever runs away is running to Hells. Whoever comes and surrenders, he should be in safety and in peace, absolute light and eternal life for eternity.

We are asking forgiveness and blessings from Allah Almighty. For the honour of the most honoured one in His Divine Presence, Sayyidina Muhammad ﷺ—*Fateha!* ▲

24

IMAGINATION VERSUS REALITY

A'udhu bil-Lahi min ash-Shaytani-r-rajeem. Bismillahi-r-Rahmani-r-Raheem. La huwla wa la quwwata illa bil-Lahi-l-'Aliyi-l-'Azheem.

The most valuable creature on earth, which one is it?

You may say, "Mankind is the most valuable." Eh, what is their value? You can't eat them, you can't use them. A goat you can eat, you can buy, you can sell. So what is man's value?

Then you look at their creation and their attributes and their missions and their respective points, and you find that mankind are most valuable creatures on earth. That is true.

And those living now, one day their material value is going to be zero. Their value is with their spiritual being, not their material being. Material being, it is nothing, no value, but spiritual being, that is valuable in us. Therefore, when a person leaves this life—that means his spiritual being has left his material being—that material being is going to be of no value, and no one wants to be with that material being or to keep the material being of that person in their home, in their bed, in their room. No; they are quickly taking him to the cemetery to bury him because the spiritual being has just left him, just left her. No value!

And we are always being deceived by satanic agents because they are making people only to look after their material being. They are not taking any care of their real being, which is their spiritual being. And if are saying that spiritual being and material being is the same, saying, "We do not accept a spiritual being in a person," we may say, "If you claim this, that there is no spirituality in a person, why do you not keep that one when he closes his eyes and his body's movements stop. Why do you not keep him if he is only a material being but quickly take him to the cemetery — *why?* What is the difference between a living one and a passed-away one? If there is no difference between a living one and a dead one, why do you not keep him?"

If you say that they are the same, equal, a dead one and a living one, there must be something wrong with your mind. How can you say this? How can you say that a dead body and a living body are equal, that a dead one and a living one are equal?

Why are you denying that there is something else with a living one? What is your proof for saying that there is no other aspect in a man? You must be a liar, you must be an ignorant one, or you must be a deceived one.

That is for atheist people, whose beliefs are built on materialism. They are saying that there is nothing beyond the material world, and they are the biggest liars, no-mind people, most ignorant ones.

I am asking, "What mentality accepts them to be the same, a dead body and a living body?" What is their proof? They are such *shaytani* people! And everywhere this is going on in the programs of all schools, high schools, universities. They are saying only, "Material, material." Then what is the meaning of living and dying? What has happened to that dead body?

This is the biggest deception, that is making people to fall into unlimited problems. They want to bring a solution through their materialistic ideas but they aren't able. They can't bring any solution because beyond that comes another problem, and each time they want to bring solutions, ten problems become a hundred problems because it is the wrong way of solving.

"Alladhee khalaqa-l-mawta wal-hayata."[203] Allah Almighty, the Creator, is saying, *"I create a living body or a dead body. By My divine order, a material being stands up and is clothed as a living being. If My order does not come on a material thing, that material thing can't be a living one."* You can shape so many statues or *heykals*, figures. Yes, you can make them, but you can't give that secret of life to that stone.

"You are keeping in your museums hundreds of figures of stone, of gold, of *bakır*, copper, of every kind. You can shape them but you aren't able to give the secret of life to them. I am the only One who gives My order to non-living elements to come and be alive, to be able to look and see, to hear and listen, to touch and know, to walk, to grasp, to do. That is My divine secret that I grant to those originally material beings. *I* make them, by My order, to stand up and walk and do, but you—*you* can't do this. You can shape

---

[203] *"He who created death and life."* (67:2)

rocks as a man, as a lion, as an ox, as a eagle, as a wolf, as a bear, but you can't clothe them in what I am clothing them because you are creatures. I am the Creator. I can do that. You can't do it!

"And you who I clothed from My secret order to be alive, I am giving a time limit for your life. When that time finishes, you must fall down, as when you put a *pil* or battery for some instrument and that battery works in that recorder or other instrument for a limited time. When it finishes, that instrument is going to be dead, finished.

"I am that One who gives life to each one of the smallest beings that you call microscopic creatures. *I dress them with life.*" *Subhanallah,* glory be to the Lord of Heavens! "If I do not dress those ones with life, they can't be alive. They will stay on the level of materiality."

Therefore, all teaching systems, teaching methods now in the twenty-first century, they are a hundred per cent wrong and just built on lies and on imagination. And when you see these coming, new generations, their understanding is a wrong understanding, and wrong understanding is the sources of troubles.

As many people as there may be alive, you can't find two persons' imagination to be the same. Everyone has an imagined world and they live in that imagined world.[204] You live in your world, he lives in his imagined world—

---

[204]That is, our understanding is based on our minds' individual perceptions and conclusions (imaginations) which have no basis in reality but nevertheless form our world view.

everyone. They are so different. Billions of kinds of imagined worlds, so that you can't enter his imagination and he can't enter your imagined world. It is only for you.

Therefore, man is single; each one is single. "Oh, how are we single? We are sitting with so many people."

You are single. When you take your rest in your bed, in your bedroom, at that time you feel that I am alone. "I am alone. I am a single one."

"*Yahu*, your wife is next to you!"

"No. She is just in her imagined world. You, you are in your imagined world. And you are single, as she is also single."

And when people are imagining and their thoughts are so different, they can't reach real being because of misunderstanding. When you leave off imagining, then you may understand something about yourself through heavenly knowledge. You may be able to ask about the real Being of the Creator. Then you can understand that there is a Reality that never changes.

We, daily, weekly, monthly, yearly, are changing. You are not same as in the morning now that it is noontime. You are not going to be same at *Maghrib* time.[205] You are not going to be same at nighttime; you are not going to be same tomorrow as today.

Everything that changes is not a reality, no. Reality can't change; Reality is fixed, no change coming to it. Therefore, everything changes, but the Creator never changes.

---

[205]Sunset.

And those who build their knowledge on imagining, they are not asking to reach Reality because they are not using real measures or a real balance to understand.

O creatures, when you understand, you may find a way. You may leave misunderstanding and you may make a way to true understanding. Now, for everything, you must find a way to get yourself out. *"Wa man yattaqi-Llahi yaj'al lahu makhrajan."*[206] If anyone understands the Reality of the Lord of Heavens, any time he falls into a difficult situation, He, Almighty, may open a way to take him out of it, to save him from the dirtiness and darkness and hopelessness of imagining, or to save him from the area of fear and imagination. If not, misunderstanding makes people always in darkness and in an area of hopelessness and fear, and that is the source of mankind's being in sufferings and miseries. All of them are a punishment for them and the reason for losing peace. Everywhere, no peace, because if the people of a community do not reach peace individually, collectively they can't reach peace.

And the Lord of Heavens, all glory be to Him, He knows what He created, particularly mankind. He knows what they may be in need of to be peaceful during this temporary life, and how they should reach permanent peace in eternity. If anyone keeps the advice of the Lord of Heavens, he should be happy here and Hereafter. Those who refuse, they will never save themselves from darkness, from dirtiness, from fears, from problems, from troubles. They will never leave them, here or Hereafter.

---

[206] *"And whoever is mindful of Allah, He will make a way out for him.* (65:2)

May Allah forgive me and bless you! For the honour of the most honoured one in His Divine Presence, Sayyidina Muhammad ﷺ—*Fateha*. ▲

25

ALL THINGS CHANGE EXCEPT ALLAH *TA'ALA*

A'udhu bil-Lahi min ash-Shaytani-r-rajeem. Bismillahi-r-Rahmani-r-Raheem. La hawla wa la quwatta illa bil-Lahi-l-'Aliyi-l-'Azheem.

It is an Association. Each day has a specialty, each day has a special personality. The days of the week are seven, and everyone feels in himself when it is going to be Friday, and then Saturday, Sunday, Monday, Tuesday, Wednesday, Thursday. You have a feeling that today is Saturday; it is not Friday and it is not Sunday. And another week comes, and it has also seven days.

But when we are speaking about today—it is Saturday—or we are speaking about the past Saturday, saying, "Last Saturday something happened," this Saturday is not the same as that Saturday. And it is now March. This is a new March; it is not the same as that which passed away. And then April is coming. It is a new April that belongs to 2004; it is not the same one that passed in 2003.

You, also—you are not the same one as you were last year in March, no. You are now in a new position. "*Kulli yawmin Huwa fi shan"*[207] Each day another manifestation appears, and those manifestations are countless. If you were able to calculate the number of waves on an ocean, you could reach the number of manifestations that you enter into and pass out of.

Subhanallah! People think that they are stable, that nothing changes. "I was like this yesterday and I am now the same one that I was yesterday." No! That has finished. Tomorrow you are another personality.

That belongs to the Divine Will that has programmed everyone. It is not only for mankind. Around mankind, whatever there is of creation, of creatures, they also, in every second or in every smallest unit of time, are changing.

Change is for creation. Unchangeable Existence is for the real Being of the Lord of Heavens, for the Creator. If change were to happen to Him, He couldn't be the Creator. The Creator creates, according to our limited knowledge, countless changes in every creature. Yet they are counted.

He knows! He knows where an atom is, or its nucleus, in the middle, how many particles. Each one has a personality, and where it is, He must know. *"La yakhfa 'alayhi shayun fi-l-ardi wa la fi-s-sama*[208]; there can't be anything hidden from the Creator." How could there be, while He is the Creator. If He does not create that, it can't be in existence. He must know, but we can know onlyaccording to our capacity.

Therefore, Grandshaykh, may Allah bless him, he was always saying, "The biggest mistake of mankind is that, for

---

[207] *"Each day He is at His business."* (55:29)

[208] *"Nothing in the earth nor in the heaven is hidden from Him."* (3:5)

their understanding, they are trying to bring the Existence of the Lord of Heavens, the Lord of all Creation, into their area of understanding." And look! If you get up and say to people, "I want to know about the sun and I am trying to bring it into my area of understanding, to bring it here." [Mawlana looks at a flower.] "And I am saying that it is like this flower. This is the sun."

As long as they are trying to understand about the sun, their knowledge is never going to be more than that flower. They should say only, "It looks like this." They can't approach and enter into it and see what it is, from far away saying, "Oh, the sun looks like a sunflower."

If you use your vision to understand creation, it is impossible for you. Through our sight, we can't reach a real understanding of what is in our vision. Then what about if we are saying, "Beyond the sun, beyond the stars, beyond galaxies"? But people are trying to know about creation according to their minds' capacity, and it makes them give a judgment about creation.

They are saying, "Positive knowledge,' and it is wrong knowledge. Positive knowledge—that was the new fashion in the sixteenth or seventeenth century, when they were trying to put everything into the area of positive knowledge. Now they are trying to bring everything under the microscope. If they can't bring it, they are saying, "No!"

That is the biggest mistake, and also the biggest foolishness, for those people who are claiming, "We are learned people, we are scientists, we are professors," the biggest mistake and biggest ignorance for them because you can't put *everything* under a microscope to see what it is. It is impossible, so that when we are speaking about Allah Almighty, which is the beginning of some knowledge of our Creator, we are asking to take the first step, and after it there should be countless steps, countless attempts. And when you reach some knowledge of the Lord of Heavens, He is going to be beyond that knowledge.

And as They[209] are making me speak about certain points, we are now saying that among the Lord's Essential Attributes is Unchangeable Existence, never changing. What was written in Sri Lanka on the entrance of that place? There was written, *"Allah Huwa al-an kama kan*—Allah is now as He was throughout pre-eternity."

Allah in His Eternity, throughout pre-eternity and post-eternity, is the same, never changed; *"Huwa al-an kama kan." Subhanallah! Kalamu-l-awliya*, the words of *awliya*, saints, that they are saying on that point. *Subhanallah*, unchangeable! *We* are changing. Therefore, I said to you that everything is going to be changed. Fulan has changed because he was awake and now he is going to sleep, just changed. And therefore, *"Al-idraku 'an 'adam-l-idraki idraku."*[210] That means if you want to understand about the real Being of Allah Almighty's Essence, you will reach a point at which you say, "Impossible!" *Then* you will have reached real knowledge about Him, Almighty, but finally you are saying "Impossible!"

A simple example: Do you think that an ant can bring knowledge of the real being of man to his understanding?

---

[209] The departed saints of the Nashbandi *Tariqat*, from whose inspiration Shaykh Nazim's *sohbets* proceed.

[210] The realization of our absolute lack of realization is a realization.

Perhaps it may be possible, but it is *im*possible for any creature to reach real understanding of its Creator. Finally, they will say, "It is impossible!" An ant, when it runs on the earth, may say, "Oh, if I had wings, I could reach the Heavens." And the Creator gives it wings and it tries to fly and flies, but the distance that it can fly and reach is maybe one meter or less or a little bit more—nothing! Do you think that it can reach the Heavens? Impossible!

Therefore, *"Al-idraku an darki-l-idraki idraku."* That is true, *subhanallahu-l-'Aliyu-l-'Azhim!* We must put our knowledge on a safe base. If not, it is going to be nonsense and people will fall down.

That is the biggest mistake of people living now and of those who claim, "We are learned people, we are experts, we are professors, we are scientists, we are academic people! We must know who is that Creator! We must bring that One whom you are calling 'Creator' under our microscope, or we must first look through telescopes." But then they are saying, "We are confused about which direction we must put our telescope towards—this direction, that direction. There are countless directions for bringing that One into our telescopes. Then, if we catch that One, we must bring and put Him under our microscope to look!"

Subhanallah, such foolish people! No understanding, and they claim that they are learned people. They think that they know everything! *That* is their knowledge about the Creator. Their heads are big but nothing is in them!

If a person knows about his Lord, his Creator, the more he knows, the more respect he gets for Him. Therefore, when the Prophet ﷺ was asked, "What is the most valuable effort or work or study for a person to do as servanthood to his Lord?" he said, "*Al-'ilmu bil-Lah*, to know about his Creator." That means to try to reach more knowledge so that, according to our knowledge of someone, of his perfection and power and glory, we have much more respect. A servant or a simple employee, when he goes in front of his director, closes his buttons, yes? Not for everyone, but for his director he gives much more respect because he knows about him, what he can do. And man also, according to his knowledge about his Creator, his Lord, has much more respect.

Therefore, two *rak'ats* of prayer from the Seal of Prophets, Sayyidina Muhammad ﷺ, if put on one side of the balance and on the other side of the balance all nations' prayers, the weight of two *rak'ats* from Rasul-Allah, the Seal of the Prophets, the most beloved and most honoured one, would be be much more because no one can reach his position and his knowledge about his Creator.

May Allah forgive me and forgive you, and grant His blessings for the honour of that most beloved and respected and honoured one, most glorified one in the Divine Presence, in spite of what the Wahhabis believe—*Fateha!*

It is not a prepared thing, but what They are sending, we must speak about it. We don't know, He knows. ▲

26

Concerning Black Holes

A'udhu bil-Lahi min ash-Shaytani-r-rajeem. Bismillahi-r-Rahmani-r-Raheem. La hawla wa la quwwata illa bil-Lahi-l-'Aliyyi-l-'Azheem.

I was speaking about black holes, but no one understands what I am saying. Each day is a black hole. [Mawlana makes a deep sucking sound.] From morning to evening, whatever happened today, when the sun sets, the black hole just swallows it—yes, swallows.

Where is yesterday now? [Chuckles.] The black hole took it. And today, also, when the sun sets, it will swallow today, with everything in it. *La hawla wa la quwwata illa bil-Lahi-l-'Aliyi-l-'Azheem!* People are looking to see black holes in the skies. *Yahu,* look here! Whatever is there, you may find it here.

Some of them are escaping from the black hole, but some of them are falling into it and disappearing. Today, so many million people fell into that black hole. Tomorrow they will not be in existence, finished.

The black hole is important. For thousands of years, thousands of years, people from every level have just fallen into the black hole and passed away. Where did they finish—in the cemetery? It is dust, earth; finished. Their personality disappeared, and also their material part disappeared.

We are coming now to our proud people, Europeans. They are looking from above and saying, "We are first class people. We are the head; oriental people, the tail."

Why you are fighting, O people? You are saying, "We are the most developed nations." Yes, we know. But you can't save yourself from falling into the black hole on earth. Why you are saying that oriental people's level is under your level? What is the difference between you, Western people, and Eastern people? Both of you will come one day and fall into the black hole, and you will disappear.

If you are first class people, if you are the highest level people, keep yourselves. Don't fall into the black hole; save yourselves! Why are you not using your technology to prevent yourself from falling into the black hole, each day's black hole? And no matter how many days you have, you also have, during those days, new black holes.

The black hole that belonged to yesterday passed away, taking everything and disappearing. Today, a new black hole has come and begun to take everyone, *ahyaan wa amwatan*, either living (they are also falling into it) or dead people, who are disappearing, a new black hole swallowing them every day.

Where is your science? Where is your technology, O Western people? First class, Germans; second, English; third, French; fourth, Italians. Americans are saying [parodies:] "We are first because we have so many green bank notes, dollars."

"Eh, what? But you can't prevent yourself from falling into black holes. Yes! Give *bartil, rishwat,* bribes, to the black hole!"

"No, you [the black hole] must not take anything from us. As many as you like, we may print green bank notes to give you, each day billions or trillions. Don't swallow our people because we are claiming that we are first level, first class people!"

The black hole is saying [in a black hole voice], "Oh, I have nothing to do with your dollars or euros or pounds or yens or Turkish pounds. I must take my share, and my share is the whole world that the sun is shining on and then setting. I must take them, I must swallow them!"

'Uj ibn Unuq, that huge man about whom it has come through traditional knowledge that he was a giant, when he went into the sea, the sea did not come up to his belt, and he took fish from sea and put them in the sun and ate—such a man.

Allah Almighty can do everything. Don't use your mind! Your mind is only a dot. You can't balance your Lord's, your Creator's power. Therefore, if we say such things, say "Yes!"

'Uj lived in ancient times. He was with Nuh ﷺ. And Nuh, that high level, Supreme Council prophet—Sayyidina Muhammad, Sayyidina Nuh, Sayyidina Ibrahim, Sayyidina

Musa, Sayyidina 'Isa, five supreme ones[211]—was ordered by Allah Almighty to make an ark. Then he was in need of timber, wood, and he said to 'Uj ibn Unuq, "Bring me some wood. I am going to make a ark because a flood is coming."

And 'Uj said, "If I bring it to you, what are you going to give me?"

And Nuh said, "I will make you full, no hunger."

And 'Uj said, "I begin from early morning going around to bakeries. Whatever bread they bake, I eat but I do not get full." 'Uj ibn Unuq was also like a black hole, eating everything from bakeries,

And Noah said, " I will make you full."

And 'Uj brought a big amount of wood from the forest, putting it there. "Eh! Come!" And Sayyidina Nuh ﷺ put three loaves of bread in front of 'Uj and he said, "Say *'Bismillahi-r-Rahmani-r-Raheem'* and eat!"

And 'Uj looked. "I eat all day from all the bakeries but I do not get full. What are you doing?"

"I am saying, 'Say *"Bismillahi-r-Rahmani-r-Raheem"* and eat.'"

But 'Uj said, "I will not say it, I am not going to say it."

A prophet's power must be above those ignorant ones. "O 'Uj, what are you not going to say?"

---

[211]In Islam, these five—Noah, Abraham, Moses, Jesus and Muhammad, Allah's peace and blessings be upon them all—are considered the greatest prophets, as mentioned in 33:7 and 42:13.

And 'Uj said, "I am not going to say *'Bismillahi-r-Rahmani-r-Raheem.'*"

"Now eat!"

And 'Uj ate one bread and half of the second, saying, "I am full. You are a great wizard. You played a trick on me! But I am full. You did something of wizardry that, even though I eat from bakeries every day, I do not get full.

"One bread I ate; the second I can't finish. No! I will take back all this!" He was very angry, taking away the wood he had brought and throwing it away. And from whatever remained that he did not take care of, Sayyidina Nuh built the Ark.

Now each day, black holes are going to work to swallow each day's people with their everything, till the Lord of Heavens orders that black hole, "Now, say *'Bismillahi-r-Rahmani-r-Raheem'* and finish." No more sun rising, no more sun setting, finishing. At that time, the black hole that is appointed by divine order to swallow everything each day from the earth is going to be full, and it will say, "Enough for me now! I am full."

That is our black hole which is working each day now and taking everything from the earth, and never getting full till the last moment when Allah Almighty orders the Archangel Israfil to blow the trumpet, and then time will stop, finishing.

O people, use your minds! Each day has just been swallowed for thousands of years; daily, black holes are swallowing them. And now today, you are here, and everyone is awaiting his or her fixed time to be swallowed. You should be swallowed, also, you and whatever you have.

Before a black hole swallows you, try to be for the Lord's servanthood in His Divine Presence and to be saved; because some people are going to be ground up and disappear in black holes, and they are going to be in Hells. But some of them who are servants of their Lord, the black hole will take them, swallowing, but it will be a lighted hole. The black hole will make them reach a lighted hole, and they should find the way through lighted worlds, they should find themselves in the Divine Presence forever, for eternity, for eternal life.

May Allah bless you and forgive me! For the honour of the most honoured one in His Divine Presence, Sayyidina Muhammad ﷺ—*Fateha!* ▲

27

CONCERNING THE NEED FOR A TRAINER AND GUIDE

A'udhu bil-Lahi min ash-Shaytani-r-rajeem. Bismillahi-r-Rahmani-r-Raheem. La hawla wa la quwwata illa bil-Lahi-l-'Aliyi-l-'Azheem.

Ask forgiveness, every time. At every time we are in need to ask forgiveness. And the Prophet ﷺ is the teacher for his *ummah*, for his nation. And from his time up to end of the world, all nations are from his *ummah*. No more nation for Jesus Christ, no more *ummah*, nation, for Moses, peace be on them. Now only *ummatu Muhammad*, the nation of Sayyidina Muhammad ﷺ.

He is teaching mankind because we are in need to learn. We are like wild trees that, when growing, need pruning. The root is a wild tree, and when pruning, good quality fruits are coming. Therefore, mankind, when they follow their prophets, are changinh. Their wildness goes and good characteristics come.

Rasul-Allah ﷺ was teaching his *Sahabah*, his Companions, and through his Companions, teaching his entire nation up to the Day of Resurrection, the end of the world, saying, "I ask my Lord's forgiveness seventy times daily."[212]

Allah Almighty never ordered any wrong thing to be written for him,[213] because, since he is the *qudwa*, leader or guide of all nations, all mankind, everything he did had to be correct so that anyone who wants to follow him may find an example in the Prophet and may say, "I am following him." Can't be wrong steps for prophets, particularly for the Seal of Prophets, and he was teaching, he was saying, "I am asking forgivenesss seventy times."

What was the wisdom in his saying this? Must be some wisdoms. On every level, people must ask for a higher level. You must not say that this level is enough for me; no need to improve to another level higher than this, it is okay for me. No! Allah Almighty wants His servants to come closer and to reach higher and higher levels, to enjoy themselves more because a higher level means much more pleasure and happiness and peace and enjoyment and enlightenment for servants, each time becoming higher, becoming more. Therefore, Allah Almighty wants His servants to ask for a higher level.

Even though the Seal of the Prophets, Sayyidina Muhammad ﷺ did not do anything wrong, he was also always evolving and approaching the Divine Presence more and more and more. And, if coming to a higher level, he asked forgiveness because he saw the level where he had been before, according to his understanding and glorifying when he

---

[212]Bukhari, 8:319.

[213]That is, there were no sins to be inscribed in the record of his deeds.

went up, as a *naqsan*,²¹⁴ something not suitable to be given to Allah Almighty on that level. When he went up, he was saying, *"Astaghfirullah, astaghfirullah* that before I was at a lower level. Now I am looking and I am sorry that I was on that level."

But for other people, like the ordinary people of the nation of Sayyidina Muhammad ﷺ, I think they are not doing *anything* in the right way. Everything that we are doing is in the wrong way, because if a person goes on the wrong way, every step is wrong till he changes his way from the wrong way to the right way. And Shaytan is cheating people. When they step on the right path, he says, "Come to this side to enjoy more," cheating them, and people are running to the wrong way. And for the wrong way, at every step you must ask forgiveness, you must stop your steps on the wrong way, and you must turn back to the right way, the right path. *"Thumma amanu, thumma kafaru";*²¹⁵ as Allah Almighty says. So many believers are not fixing themselves in their faith, on the right path, sometimes leaving their steps on the right way and coming and walking on the wrong way, *"Thumma amanu, thumma kafaru."* Sometimes you may find a servant walking on the right path; then after a while you may see that he has changed his position, coming to wrong way, following Shaytan.

Therefore, we are in need of training. If we are alone, by ourselves, we can't correct our steps. We are in need of guidance under the control of a trainer, *murabbi*, of a teacher, of a guide. If you do not have a guide, you can't know on

---

²¹⁴A deficiency or defect.

²¹⁵*Then they believe, then disbelieve"* (4:137), part of a verse referring to those who continue to alternate between belief and disbelief.

which way you are walking. Therefore, it is obligatory for every believer to have an *antrenör*.[216]

People playing football, football teams, have a trainer to teach them. If for playing you need a trainer, what about for those who want to reach Heavens, to reach their Lord's Divine Presence? How, without a guide, can you know what is true, correct, of your steps and what is wrong?

If it was as Wahhabi people are saying, "No need!" why did Allah Almighty send prophets? Wahhabi people are saying, "You can read, you can teach yourself by yourself," and that is *batil*, that is wrong, the wrong direction. If it were enough for a person to find his way without a guide only by looking through books, Allah Almighty would have sent *suhuf*, pages, from Heavens.[217]

Why, *why* did He send prophets? They can't understand! They can't understand what was the mission of the Prophet ﷺ, because they are square-headed people, and their square is only a millimeter square, no more. The mission of the Prophet was to be trainer, teacher and guide because we do not know anything. We must learn from our teacher.

They are saying now, "Oh, so many universities, and we are printing hundreds, thousands, of books. Take them

---

[216] Tr., trainer, coach.

[217] Here, Shaykh Nazim adds parenthetically: "Sometimes planes throw down papers from above and people are running. Fifty years ago, the first planes would sometimes come to Cyprus. They threw papers, also, for the first time after the First War. I remember those first planes coming to Cyprus. They threw down printed pages, and we looked for them to come on us, also, and we ran to them."

and learn! Why are you following shaykhs, why are you following *tariqahs*. No need! Take! We are also giving you free books!" But some people are understanding what it is written in them as "head" while they are saying "feet," and they may understand "feet" as "head," such wrong-understanding people.

Therefore, we are in need of a guide. And the Prophet ﷺ is the guide, and at every time we are in need. If no necessity for teachers, why are you establishing so many universities and bringing so many professors? *Why?* Let students learn by themselves! Make libraries (they have so many libraries); everyone can bring a book and can look, can teach himself. Why bring teachers, professors? No answer, because they are a millimeter-square headed people. They can't be outside the square. Allah Allah!

This fine point makes Islam to be elevated or to disappear. Those people who are claiming that we are the guides of Islam, they are not accepting our way, the way of *Ahla 's-Sunnah wa 'l-Jama'ah*.[218] They are saying, "We are Salafi people,"[219] and they are claiming that there is no need for guides. It is only a very fine difference. This side is the correct side, that side is the wrong side. And for that purpose, for that reason, we must follow guides; we must ask for

---

[218]The People of the Prophet's *Sunnah* [Practice] and Congregation, i.e., Sunni Muslims, whom the Prophet ﷺ mentioned as being that group among Muslims who would be saved on the Last Day.

[219]A strict, puritanical group who follow literal interpretations, reject spiritual understandings, *awliya,* Sufism, and the four schools of Sunni jurisprudence *(madhdhahib)*.

teachers[220], and they may show us the wrong steps or the correct steps.

If you lose your correct steps, you will fall down, finished; no chance to go up. And we seeing that now in our days, the twenty-first century, the Muslim world is running to be on the Salafis' wrong way because Salafi people are working on our egoistic characteristic. They are defending, they are taking the side of egos' characteristic, *yushaji'a ahli-l-hawa*, going with people's egoistic characteristic.

Ego's characteristic is that it never likes to follow anyone. To justify this bad characteristic, they are saying, "No! We are not in need of any trainer." That means of a shaykh or *'alim*.[221] "No need! We are doctors. You can teach yourself and you can find your way."

Yahu! A sail boat, if it does not have a compass and map, can't move through the ocean. How are you saying that only a sail boat is enough for you? Take your sail boat and hold on to this wheel! In every direction, you are free in that ocean, so why are you taking a compass and a map? No; you must be free everywhere in this ocean, in any direction you go. And you will never reach your goal. You are in need of a compass and a map, and now radar, also, to show.

They are denying everything about training *mu'assasa*,[222] training foundation, while Allah Almighty is saying, "Wal-takun minkum ummatun yad'una ila-l-khairi wa yamuruna bi-l-

---

[220] That is, the four *imams* who founded the four schools of Sunni jurisprudence, plus the true shaykhs of *tariqahs*.

[221] Islamic scholar.

[222] Training foundation, base.

*m'arufi wa yanhawna 'ani-l-munkar."*²²³ That is, you must keep some learned people to teach you what are correct steps and what are wrong steps. But now they are the first deniers of that verse, and saying, "People can learn by themselves and they can use their *safinah*, sail boats, throughout this life. In every direction they may move. Doesn't matter!" And they are doing the worst, worst thing; they are doing their worst to Islam. Even the non-Muslim world is not doing that to Islam.

May Allah forgive us! Therefore we are asking forgiveness because, mostly, if we sail through this ocean by ourselves, it is so difficult if we do not use a compass and map—so difficult to find where you are going, on the wrong way or the right way. We must know if we are on the correct steps. You must ask someone if they are true, right steps or wrong steps.

And we are in need also to ask forgiveness. That is the reason. If, each day, the Prophet was saying seventy times *"Astaghfirullah!"* what about for you, for me, for others? Seventy million times is even a small amount! Say *"Astaghfirullah!"* at least seventy times each day and keep a guide for yourself. Beware of being without a guide—beware! You may be lost, you may just lose everything here and Hereafter. Keep to the right path. You should be in safety here and Hereafter.

But, as we said, Salafi people are addressing our egos and making egos to be proud. You see that all of them, if you want to speak to them about their religion, about their

---

²²³*"And let there be among you a community summoning to the good, enjoining the right and forbidding the wrong."* (3:104)

beliefs, are saying, "I know! I am not in need of listening or learning from you," because the heaviest position for ego is to be under someone's control. Ego never accepts to be a student, a learner—no; always asking to be a learned one. "I know. I am not in need of listening to you."

And that is the position, the general view of the whole world. Everyone is doing their worst, giving the wrong orders to people. And the blame is coming on Islam, and they are saying "Fundamentalist," but it does not concern Islam. Fundamentalism concerns a group of people who are under the control of Shaytan and devils. A person can't be a fundamentalist if he is not a devil. Devils they are fundamentalists but Muslims are not fundamentalists. It is a big lie that people want to blame Islam. No, it is not for true Islam. No fundamentalism in Islam!

May Allah send us a true guide to save us from the hands of devils who are the representatives of Shaytan. May Allah forgive me and bless you! For the honour of the most honoured one in His Divine Presence, Sayyidina Muhammad ﷺ—*Fateha!* ▲

28

HUMANKIND WANTS TO REACH SOMEWHERE

A'udhu bil-Lahi min ash-Shaytani-r-rajeem. Bismillahi-r-Rahmani-r-Raheem. La hawla wa la quwwata illa bil-Lahi-l-'Aliyi-l-'Azheem.

What is servanthood? Servanthood is for a servant to declare, to say to his Lord, "O my Lord, You are my Lord, You are my Creator. You have brought me from nothingness to be visible in existence," because there is no place in existence to be independent with your being. Where can you go? You may go with your physical being, or, if you are prepared to use it and to move, with you spiritual power.

Man has been granted two powers. One is our physical being and whatever power belongs to our physical being. We use that power of your physical being that develops. Beginning with our coming from our mother's womb, that physical power begins to increase. And when we reach our maturity, we see that we are now powerful, we may move.

And after that, people think that it is going to continue for years and years, and to keep increasing as our age increases, but it is not so. We reach a limit of growing, and when we reach that point, our growth and development stops, and our power reaches its last point.

Going up, up, up is not unending, no. When we reach a certain level, our physical being's power begins to reduce, to be less and less and less, and we reach a point when we feel that our physical power is not going to carry us, not going to be enough for our movements. We say, "Come and hold my hand," or, "Bring my stick," or, "Hold me from this side, also." What has happened to you? Your physical being is going down. Its power getting less and less and less.

This momentum belongs to our physical being, making us move throughout East and West, from North to South, through continents, through oceans, to climb mountains, and to reach the Poles. We want to reach *somewhere*. And that is a secret desire; its seeds are planted in our physical being. We have a habit of liking to see what is behind this wall or what is in each continent—what is there. If we reach a place, we say, "We must go to Africa, also, to see what is *there*." Our physical being wants to know. And we aren't able to explain this habit. *Why?* That secret desire always wants to do some research, looking at what is there, asking to find something. That is our physical being's momentum.

And they are looking and they are not finding any place empty. They are finding every place full, full of something—full of unknown creatures, full of unknown things. We want to find, and Shaytan is making man to search, to look for an empty place.

What is the real aim? To find an empty place where we can be in safety from death, to find a place where death can't reach us. We want to be free in that place. But everywhere men are going and reaching, death also reaches.

It has come to us through traditional knowledge that once, in the time of prophets, King Solomon, Prophet Suleiman ﷺ was sitting on his throne, where people could come and look at him; they could ask, they could visit him. Prophets' doors are never locked. It is a divine attribute.[224]

People are asking to find an open place where there is no one who can control them, asking to be free there from their real aspects being taken by death, to be free there from the Angel of Death's reaching them. That is the real, deep and secret desire of people—to move like this, like that. But even though they are going everywhere, wherever they go, they are finding that it is same. An empty place, no—no empty place where they do not find there the Angel of Death, everywhere finding that divine power. That means that everywhere that mankind moves across this earth, climbing mountains, going through deserts, sailing on oceans, going through jungles, they will not find a place empty or not controlled by someone. This our physical being's momentum.

---

[224]Here, Mawlana adds: "Therefore, the Holy Ka'bah in Makkatu-l-Mukarramah traditionally has forty entrances, with no doors—no. At any time, anyone should enter without being asked, "Why are you coming, what are you doing?" But now Wahhabi people are making every trouble for visiting people, pilgrims. They are searching them to enter.

It is open because that is the House of the Lord, and the House of the Lord should never be closed by doors. They built a huge building and put big entrances, big [closable] doors, and that is against heavenly rules. And at the beginning of the fifteenth century *Hijra*,[224] on the first day of 1400, some rebels entered it, and the government authorities closed the doors and killed all of them.[224] They did that against heavenly rules, putting doors to close. And those rebel people never expecting that someone may come inside, and close the doors and shoot them. Therefore, to be open, it is Allah Almighty's Divine attribute.

Everywhere He is present; His Presence fills every place. "That is My own territory," Allah Almighty is saying. "O mankind and jinn, I see that you are looking for some crack, some exit to get out." You are looking in space, if you can find some ways to escape, and looking through cracks in the earth, to go into those cracks and to disappear, so that the Angel of Death can't reach you."

They are not finding it. They are looking up to get out. Our material being moves within a very small distance, asking for an empty space to get out, not to be controlled, not to be reached by death. But they will never find a space, a place on earth or a space in the skies, where the Angel of Death's control does not reach.

King Solomon's doors were open, couldn't be closed. And there was one person who frequently came and visited him.

One day he was sitting with King Solomon, and the Lord of Heavens, the Lord of Creation, sent the Archangel of Death, Archangel 'Izra'il, to take back that one's soul. Archangel 'Izra'il reached there, and he also sat next to King Solomon, and he was looking at that one. And that person said to King Solomon, "O my Lord's prophet, that one is looking at me too seriously, in astonishment."

And King Solomon asked, "Do you know who that one is?"

"I don't know."

"He is Archangel 'Izra'il, come to take your soul."

"O my Lord's prophet, please send me to India! Save me from his hands!"

"I will," King Solomon said, and he ordered the air to take that one to India. In just a moment, he stepped into India, but the archangel had reached there before him and he took his soul.

Then Archangel 'Izra'il came again to King Solomon, and King Solomon asked, "Why were you looking so keenly at that servant of the Lord? "

"O *Nabi-Allah*,[225] O Solomon, I was ordered to take his soul in India and I was surprised that he was sitting with you. How could it be? And then you ordered him to be in India. I was there to take his soul."

Therefore, no one can escape. Men want to escape. Really, that is the secret desire of every living one, not to die. But they are searching, looking around everywhere to find a door, an entrance to go into and close it on Archangel 'Izra'il so that he will not reach them. But they can never find such a place.

Spiritually there is movement for ourselves, but it is not for everyone. Everyone is not prepared to go around in the Heavens. If they are prepared and move, they will reach from one heaven to another heaven. But they will never find any space where there is not the power of the Lord of Heavens, no empty place that Allah Almighty does not control. Nothing can be out of His control.

---

[225] Prophet of Allah.

O people, leave that ignorance! Come and say, "*La ilaha illa-Llah.* O our Lord, we are Your servants." Surrender to Him, to put you in His divine safety and to be eternal ones for eternity. Why are you not saying it? You should be taken, as that person was taken from the presence of King Solomon to India. Therefore, you can't find any place, anywhere, that is not under the control of the Lord of Heavens or not under His hegemony or out of His dominion, divine dominion.

May Allah forgive me! Therefore, you must try as much as you can to be a good servant. Don't waste your life. Don't waste your very valuable breath and life, and lose everything. Look after your life! Mankind must change their life routines now for their safety, for their happiness here and Hereafter.

May Allah send us some of His lions from His Divine Presence, to take away from the earth wolves, bears, foxes, jackals, scorpions and dragons, and to kill devils and defeat and destroy the *sultanat* of Satan, to make world clean for His servants. May Allah grant us that, for the honour of the most honoured one in His Divine Presence—*Fateha!* ▲

29

THE IMPORTANCE OF SEEKING SPIRITUAL PERFECTION

A'udhu bil-Lahi min ash-Shaytani-r-rajeem. Bismillahi-r-Rahmani-r-Raheem. La hawla wa la quwwata illa bil-Lahi-l-'Aliyi-l-'Azheem.

A teacher doesn't get to be tired when he teaches little ones. Yes; if he gets tired, he isn't able to teach anyone.

You may repeat something that is necessary to be learned, but the important point in learning is practicing what you learn. You must try to practice it, not to keep it in your mind. It is not enough. Learning, what you have learned, must come to an *acting* level. If you get medicine from a physician but do not use it, putting it on the table and looking at it, you can't get any benefit. You may say, "This is so bitter. That is such a bad-smelling one, I can't take it. That is an injection. I never use it, it gives me trouble." What is the benefit of having medicines and not using them?

All prophets came to teach people the ways of perfection. We come with a perfect material or physical being. but it is not enough to be perfect in our physical being. What

Almighty Allah wants for everyone is perfection in their spiritual position. Therefore, He ent prophets to teach man the ways of perfection.

As grandshaykhs[226] say, as well as knowledgeable people, a person's outward appearance or physical being is going to be clear after forty days in the womb. That perfection grows, grows, and then our mother gives birth, and day by day, year by year, we grow up. But the real perfection that we have been asked to reach, it is not easy to reach that level. The level of spiritual perfection is difficult. Perhaps it needs forty years, thirty years, twenty years or ten years.

If you do not ask for that perfection, your level is the level of animals, the lowest level of creation. No difference between that one and that ox, between that one or that dog—no, because every creature has material or physical perfection. A cat is in its perfection as a cat; an ox is perfect among its kind as an ox, and in their physical being, men are in perfection at the same level as other creatures. But we have been asked to reach spiritual perfection, while other creatures are only created for mankind during this life so that man may get benefit from them.

Animals are created *for the service of* mankind. When they have fulfilled the main purpose for which they were created, they finish; no responsibility on them. But men are not created to give their physical being *for the service of* any creature, no. Every creature *is* created for man, but man *is* not created for them.

---

[226] High-ranking *awliya*, Muslim saints.

A question whose answer is important to be known: Yes, everyone knows that men are not created for other creatures; *m*en are not going to be servants to the animal world, no. But the whole animal world has been created for mankind, to use them as they like. The whole animal world *is* under the command and under the *wishes* of mankind, but *n*ever is man going to be the servant of animals, no.

Yes, you may keep animals, *and y*ou may give your service to them to make them ready for your service. If you do not look after them when they are in need, they are not going to give any benefit to you. Therefore, we are serving animals, when they are in need, for ourselves, for our own benefit. No one is going to be a servant of animals except for the purpose that they should be servants to you.

But mankind's position is a different position and it is a different service that has been asked from mankind. If all creatures are servants to mankind, there must also be some different service for men to Someone, and that is our servanthood to our Creator. Servanthood, that is the difference of our position from other creatures. They are servants to us and we are servants to Allah Almighty.

Then, when we are servants to our Creator, the Lord of Heavens, our servanthood is not through our physical being. We have been asked to reach never-ending spiritual perfection that is for our Creator. Our physical being is only for a short time, a very short time, and its perfection is only for keeping our souls in, but it is not a perpetual being. Our physical being is going to be dust. But the perfection of our spiritual being, that is something else. And prophets came and taught people how they should reach spiritual perfection.

If you reach that perfection, you are the most fortunate one. Those who do not take any care, their position is going to be worse than animals' position because animals are finally going to be dust and disappear. But mankind, those who do not take any care of their spirituality, their physical being is not going to be dust except in their graves.

Then it will come into the Divine Presence on the Day of Resurrection. Our physical being is going to be there, not going to disappear like animals' beings. And those who neglected their spirituality should be forever in troubles, in misery, in fires that burn them because they never took care of their spiritual perfection. Those who took care of their spiritual perfection, they should be happy with a new beginning, with a new structure, with a new being. They should be in unknown paradises that they only heard about before, and their perfection should continue in Paradise, also.

I am sorry to say that people now care only about their physical being. They want to make their physical being more perfect, but more perfection for our physical being is impossible. After a while, after a period, after a short time, our physical being's perfection is slowly going to come down, come down, come down, and going to be at the point of zero, dying. Our physical being, no matter how much you try to give it perfection with what people now are trying to do for that purpose, everything is still only for that physical being. The only care for all the world—learned people, physicians and technology, everything—is just directed at our physical being's perfection and to make that perfection continue and last forever. And it is impossible.

They know that, but they are running after it. Every *jahd*, effort, of learned people is directed at our physical beings' perfection. And it is not continuous perfection, going up, up to forty years, and then beginning to come down. That perfection that we have increases up to forty years. After that, whatever you do, it is impossible to turn it back as we were forty years or thirty years or twenty years or fifteen years ago; no. The perfection of people's physical beings, if nothing from outside comes on him or her,[227] is only up to forty years. Then, whatever medicine, whatever practices, whatever eating or drinking they use will never give more perfection after that age. Must come down, and coming to the point of zero, finishing.

One week or ten days ago, TV was showing a navy dreadnought, a Russian warship, that was working by nuclear power. And they were in fear. They were taking every care for that ship, but they were not taking care of that nuclear power and they were afraid that there would be an explosion. There was an unseen power there, and they weren't able to stop it, also, because when the time came, it was going to explode and make it nothing.

That is losing everything that we were granted for reaching perfection in our physical being. We may give every care, attention and concern for our physical being, but we are not taking any care of that power that makes our physical being move, work, and live.

Now mankind, also, are thinking that our physical being makes us be in life. No! That secret power inside is like

---

[227] An illness or accident, etc.

nuclear power. If we do not take care, it is going to explode and your physical being is going to be zero, nothing. If you take it without an explosion, it is protected and can be used another time.[228] When people come on the Day of Resurrection, that power will come with them, but those who destroyed themselves will finish. Those who took care of themselves, of that secret power, they should be happy.

People now are not taking care of that unseen power that makes a man to move, to live, to do everything, and that point needs development and improvement to reach the way of perfection. Therefore, Allah Almighty sent, from His Divine Presence from Heavens, some of His chosen servants who have been dressed in that secret power to arrange the lives of people on earth for reaching their real perfection. But people are running after material perfection, and material perfection is going to be the reason of curses now in the twenty-first century, and the whole world now, it is just ready to explode. Day by day, the whole world is now waiting for the one day, the one hour, when it is going to explode and destroy everything that mankind has established for their physical improvement or their physical pleasure, going to finish. That is coming now. It is called "Armageddon," written about in the Old Testament, the New Testament, and also it is indicated in the seal of holy books, Qur'an al-Karim.

May Allah forgive us and bless those who are asking for the honour of being servants to their Lord, and make us with those people who are asking for that honour. There is no honour, no safety, no happiness or peace here or Hereaf-

---

[228]That is, if you master it during this life, it will be resurrected with you on the Last Day for your use in the eternal life.

ter without Allah Almighty's dressing His servants in that honoured dress. May Allah grant us that, for the honour of the most honoured one in His Divine Presence, Sayyidina. Muhammad ﷺ—*Fateha!* ▲

30

THE REAL GOAL OF THE NAQSHBANDI *TARIQAH*

A'udhu bil-Lahi min ash-Shaytani-r-rajeem. Bismillahi-r-Rahmani-r-Raheem. La hawla wa la quwwata illa bil-Lahi-l-'Aliyi-l-'Azheem.

The Most Distinguished Naqshbandi Order is now the only way that working as a *tariqah*.[229] Other *tariqahs'* ways have just stopped because there us no maintenance for them.[230] They have been left, and it is difficult to move in them and to reach our goals. And the main goal that we must take our utmost care of is to reach Allah, nothing else, because, in any case, you will finally reach His Divine Presence.

---

[229] *Tariqah/tariqat* ('way' or 'path') refers to Sufi orders.

[230] Meaning that currently, in all *tariqahs* except the Naqshbandiyya, there are no longer shaykhs whose appointment is authorized. That is, the current shaykhs are either self-appointed or appointed by a predecessor who was not authorized to pass on the leadership of the *tariqah*, and who may be good, righteous men but not *awliya* (saints).

Therefore, our efforts here—what we are doing to reach imitation goals or imaginary goals—are not taking us anywhere because they are not real, true goals for mankind. Can't be! All the goals that we are trying to put our efforts towards reaching, all of them belong to our material world. And the material world, even if you reach all material aspects, material values, material treasures, is not going to be with you when you leave this life. It will not give you anything, and your effort is going to be lost, wasted. You will really have reached nothing.

Instead, the real goal must be beyond our material being. Beyond our material being comes spiritual being, spiritual aspects and spiritual values that are beyond our physical life and beyond our material being. And we must look at our goals: for what we are giving our utmost care, for which thing we are giving everything that we have been granted spiritually and physically, and with what we are wasting it; we must look at that point. And we are seeing that the majority, perhaps now ninety-nine per cent and more of people, want to reach imitation goals that belong to our physical being.

When our physical being finishes and vanishes, its goal will also finish and vanish, disappear. When your physical being disappears, its efforts and goals are finished; when you bury a person in the graveyard, *everything* is finished. Where did that one's efforts and works and activities go—where? Disappeared, finished! When burying a person, everything that belonged to his material being just finishes. Therefore, material aspects can't be our real goal.

Our real, true goal is to find the way to reach our Lord's Divine Presence. If you give your effort to that goal, it is a *real* goal. When you leave this physical and material life, you will not lose your real goal, you will reach your real goal. Our real goal never has any interest in our physical being, not taking any interest. If taking an interest, it would have carried our material being with it, also. But it never carries it, leaving it to be buried, leaving it to be dust under the earth, underground.

And that is the reason we are trying to teach or to show people a real aspect as a goal, since most people do not think about it because they are surrounded by material aspects, and material aspects never let them be interested in what is beyond those aspects. And they are imprisoned by material desires, physical desires, physical enjoyments. They want that, wanting to reach more and more; but every time, they are becoming less, less, less, and at the point of zero they are finishing.

Now, in our traditional knowledge that our Grandshaykh was giving, there were forty-one *tariqahs*, each *tariqah* trying to carry people to their real aspects. But for a long time now, there has been no maintenance of forty *tariqahs* because the real authority in those *tariqahs* has passed away and the *tariqah* has become weaker, weaker, weaker, and now no one is able to continue or maintain those ways.

Therefore, those who are coming and working through those *tariqahs*, it is so difficult for them to reach their real goals because no more authorized guides for them, no guidance. Only the Most Distinguished Naqshbandi Order always has maintenance, and it is ready and prepared for everyone who is asking for the real goal that belongs to their spirituality and spiritual worlds, spiritual desires, spiritual being, and who are asking know about the reality of reaching their real goals. We are now living in a time when only the Most Distinguished Naqshbandi Order is ready to take people from the darkness of materiality, to carry them away and bring them to a lighted world, to look and see, through those heavenly lights, their future, their goals, their promise.[231]

To make all mankind remember their promise, the Naqshbandi Order is sufficient because the Naqshbandi Order is calling people to keep the promise that they made when we were in the spiritual world, guiding us to our promise in the Divine Presence, when we said, "O our Lord, You are our Lord. At every time, we want to be with You, to accept Your commands and to keep Your holy orders for reaching Your Divine Presence, and to be Your sincere servants in Your Divine Presence." That is all.

We have been called to keep our promise to Allah Almighty in the spiritual world that we were going to keep ourselves for reaching His Divine Presence and being His honoured servants. We are in need, for that purpose, of teachers who can teach us. And all prophets were teachers and reminders for people. "O people, you gave your oath to your Lord on the Day of Promises that you were going to be *His* servants only, not anyone else's." And all prophets and

---

[231]Referrring to the Day of Promises, mentioned in 7:172: *"And [mention] when your Lord took from the children of Adam—from their loins—their descendants and made them testify concerning themselves, [saying to them], 'Am I not your Lord?' They said, 'Yes, we testify to it.'"* The question, *"Am I not your Lord?"* and the affirmative answer to it means that all humanity-to-come confirmed their acceptance of Allah's Lordship and Sovereignty, and their intention to be true to that affirmation by being sincere, obedient servants to Him.

their inheritors, *awliya*, have been trying to make people remember that oath and promise so that we may move towards our Lord's Divine Presence.

But people are running away. When they run away, curses run after them and troubles surround them and problems face them, so that there is no rest for them day or night. Particularly if a person is in a high position, in which whole nations are under his command, he has many more troubles and problems than others. And it is impossible for one person to bring solutions for countless problems or to take away sadness and troubles and miseries and sufferings from people. It is impossible.

The way our grandshaykhs used to awaken mankind was Association. When they sat with people, their first goal was to make attenders think about their oath and promise. Most people do not know about their promise. This is a reminder for common people to think about their promise in the Divine Presence, so that, when they think about real obedience, you see that they come to the way of praying *and* making the first and most important goal for men living on earth to find their way to their Creator, Allah Almighty.

It is not easy, it is not easy, but it is not impossible. It is only not easy, but it is not impossible. You must carry a burden, a heavy burden, to learn and to follow the ways reaching to the Divine Presence. Day by day, you may learn, and you may move step by step to the Divine Presence of the Lord of Heavens, our Creator.

May Allah forgive me and grant to you, by His blessings, not to be deceived by Satan and satanic groups. Every place is full of satanic groups. They never like a person who is interested in spirituality, and they want all people only to be interested in materialism. And materialism brings atheism, atheists, who say, "No Creator!"

If there is no Creator, I am saying, a hundred years ago, who was present in this place? And now you are here. Do you think that you brought yourself into existence? If you can do that, why do you not keep yourself in this life permanently? And that is a proof.

If they say, "No Creator, everyone creates himself," we are saying, "Why do you not continue to keep your physical structure? If you can do that, repair or maintain your body to continue in this life." But they never think about what we are saying, and to think is the key that opens the treasures of realities.

May Allah forgive us and grant us good understanding. For the honour of the most honoured one in His Divine Presence, Sayyidina. Muhammad ﷺ—*Fateha!* ▲

31

MATERIAL ASPECTS NEVER GIVE SATISFACTION

Absolute perfection is only for Allah, never changing. Stability, absolute stability is only for Allah, without any change, no. From pre-eternity to post-eternity, there is no one to make Him move or to change His position, no. *Allahu Akbar!*

A'udhu bil-Lahi min ash-Shaytani-r-rajeem. Bismillahi-r-Rahmani-r-Raheem. By the name of Allah, All-Mighty, All-Merciful, Most Beneficent and Most Munificent. Glory be to Him! We have been ordered to know about Him, Almighty.

Adam ﷺ was created and settled in Paradise. And he was carrying on his back all of his descendants' DNA, of which no one's is ever the same as anyone else's. They say, "We are analyzing and researching and finding that this belongs to Fulan." But his DNA is not a hundred per cent the same as his father's or mother's. No, it must be changed.

Adam was carrying those seeds of all his descendants, but when you say "seeds," it would be impossible for them to be seen even under the most powerful microscope. Never! Millions of them can't be seen. And they are between the material and non-material area, or their material aspects belong to the material world as well as reaching the spiritual world, also. If they belonged only to the material world, they would have no life.

When we say 'life,' it means what is understood by us. They are dead ones; what we call 'living' ones are not alive, Everything that belongs to the material world is also alive, but its life is not like our lives.[232]

Therefore, Adam ﷺ was carrying on his back the material particles that were the seeds of mankind. The seeds held material beings' smallest representatives. And if the secret power that belongs to Heavens did not touch them and come on them, they would not be living ones—such small ones, small living parts or the smallest living figures, seeds of mankind. Allah Almighty is looking and seeing the personality of everyone in that, and giving that power to the Seal of the Prophets. He can see. And according to their light or the enlightenment in their hearts, prophets and *awliya*, saints, are looking and seeing the life in those seeds.

Adam ﷺ was carrying all of them. He was in Paradise, and he was carrying all of his descendants. And as you see or hear or read or know about his descendants, from the beginning up to today, mostly they are violent ones, disobedient ones and rebellious ones. Their interest is not in their

---

[232] Meaning that to be in existence, every single creation, from the largest galaxy to the tiniest sub-sub atomic particle, must be granted a quality of "being alive" from the Divine Power Ocean, without which it cannot emerge from the domain of absolute non-existence (*'adaman mutlaq*) to the domain of existence (*al-wujud*).

Creator and His obedience and His pleasure; their greatest interest is in material aspects. Therefore, Adam's descendants whom he was carrying made Adam ﷺ look around Paradise.

He was happy, looking at Paradise and what was in it. And he was feeling enjoyment and pleasure in his manly structure, his manly personality that was his material figure, working through divine power. He looked around and he was so happy, enjoying.

But although he was going around, he was not in real satisfaction. He was looking and saying, "I am not fully satisfied," till Allah Almighty, in less than a second or a smaller unit of time, made him doze, and Adam lost himself within himself, like this. And in that unit of time, Allah Almighty created Eve with such beauty that no one can reach her beauty.

When Adam ﷺ looked and saw her, he said, "Oh, now Paradise is full!" He had reached satisfaction, and he said, "Come to me!"

She said, "No. You come!"

And Adam ﷺ went. Yes! If I had been there, I would have gone, also. [Laughter.] And Adam ﷺ was in his full power, not used.

Look! The thing for which Adam ﷺ got up and went to Eve—his descendants, who were asking for satisfaction only through materiality, made Adam look and go to find satisfaction with her. Otherwise, his satisfaction must be *"Ala bi-dhikri-Llahi tatma'innu-l-qulub."*[233]

---

[233] *"Unquestionably, in the remembrance of Allah hearts are assured."* (13:28)

He would not have gone to look at Eve or anything else because he was looking at his Lord. Finding satisfaction with Eve was from his descendants whom he was carrying on his back, whose whose interest was in materiality and material aspects or material desires, making him go. Otherwise, Adam really would not have looked at Eve. He was asking for the Lord of Paradise, the Lord of Heavens.

Therefore, when he lost his chance to be in Paradise he was crying. He was crying when he was sent to earth, crying. He was not crying for Eve; he was crying because he had lost his Lord's Presence, his Lord's pleasure. Therefore, at that time he understood that his rebellious descendants had made him run to Eve, and when he ran to Eve, the Lord was not happy.

The Lord of Heavens was not happy for Adam to look at anyone else and to look at Eve, but it was those rebellious descendants, whose desires were only materiality, who did this. Otherwise, Adam ﷺ was innocent, innocent; he could not do anything wrong.[234] But because he had all his descendants, *mu'min, kafir*,[235] everyone with him, they made him fall into that wrong action, *khata*, mistake.

It was a mistake. He did not make *hawa*[236] by himself. As wind sends a sail boat, he was sent to Eve, and from Eve to that forbidden tree. When coming to earth, he cried for three hundred years because he had lost the familiarity of

---

[234]It is an Islamic belief that although prophets were capable of making mistakes, they were free of sins.

[235]Belivers and unbelievers.

[236]Desire, love, passion.

his Lord's Divine Presence. He cried for that; not crying for Eve or anyone else, no.

The biggest mistake of people now is that they are running after materiality, and materiality never gives satisfaction. Even if it is more and more and more, it never gives satisfaction. Allah Almighty is saying, "If you are asking for satisfaction, you can find it with Me. When you are going to be in My Divine Presence, you will just have reached satisfaction, peace and enjoyment, unlimited pleasure with Me, because the one who is with Me finds eternal enjoyment, increasing enjoyment, every time, every day, up to eternity. Eternal enjoyment for you!"

People now are on wrong way because they want satisfaction, contentment, happiness and peace within themselves through material aspects. But the biggest teaching is Adam's situation in Paradise and what happened to him. It is enough for all nations, for all of his descendants, to understand. But they are *not* understanding and they are deceived by Shaytan, and satanic teachings are making people fall into miseries, sufferings, problems, endless troubles. And the biggest trouble-maker is Shaytan and his followers, devils.

I am sorry to say that now, everywhere, Shaytan's representatives, devils, are in power. And they are forcing mankind to move, to follow shaytanic teachings and reject heavenly teachings, so that there is no good sign now for their future.

They are going to fall into such a bad condition! Now it is nothing, but in the future that is approaching, they should taste the punishment of their wrong steps. And the whole world's people, till they change their steps, leaving satanic teachings, are never going to be happy here or Hereafter. That is the heavenly teaching in the Old Testament, New Testament, Holy Qur'an and *Zabur*, Psalms, of Sayyidina David ﷺ. The *khulasa*, summary or, more than summary, essence—the essence of holy books is this. As long as men are running after material aspects, they can't reach any satisfaction or pleasure—no, no, no, no!

Mankind must change their ways. But I see that it is going to be impossible with our leaders or governments. They aren't able. Even religious people who claim to belong to Christianity, Judaism and even Islam do not have not enough capacity to change people's directions from the wrong way to the right way. And I am only asking from Allah Almighty to send us some of His servants who are supported by heavenly powers. Otherwise, it is impossible for billions of people to be changed from the wrong way.

May Allah forgive us! And within a short time, I am looking for those ones to be sent. When it is evening, I am asking to reach them before morning, I am so thirsty to reach them to save mankind from the hands of devils and the satanic kingdom.

May Allah forgive us and grant us those ones. For the honour of the most honoured one in His Divine Presence, Sayyidina Muhammad ﷺ—*Fateha!* ▲

Glossary

Abu Bakr as-Siddiq—the closest of the Prophet's Companions and his father-in-law, who shared the Hijrah with him. After the Prophet's death, he was chosen by consensus of the Muslims as the first caliph or successor to the Prophet. He is known as one of the most saintly of the Prophet's Companions.

'Abdul-Khaliq al-Ghujdawani—the eleventh grandsheikh of the Naqshbandi *tariqah*, one of the Khwajagan of Central Asia.

Abu Hanifa—founder of one of the four schools of Islamic jurisprudence, the Hanafi *madhhab*.

Abu Yazid Bistami—Bayazid Bistami, a great ninth century *wali* and Naqshbandi master.

Adab—good manners, proper etiquette.

Adhan—the call to prayer.

Ahl al-Bayt—People of the House, that is, the family of the Holy Prophet ﷺ.

Ahl ad-dunya—people of the world, i.e., those who are attached to its life and pleasures.

Akhirah—the Hereafter, the Eternal Life.

Alhamdulillah—praise be to Allah, praise God.

Allahu akbar—God is the Most Great.

Amir (pl., 'umara)—chief, leader, head of a nation or people.

Anbiya (plural of **nabi**)—prophets.

'Aql—mind, intellect, intelligence, reason, discernment.

'Arafat—a vast plain outside Mecca where pilgrims gather for the principal rite of Hajj.

'Arif—knower; in the present context, one who has reached spiritual knowledge of his Lord.

Ar-Raheem—the Mercy-Giving, Merciful, Munificent, one of Allah's ninety-nine Holy Names

Ar-Rahman—the Most Merciful, Compassionate, Beneficent, the most often repeated of Allah's Holy Names.

Ashhadu an la ilaha illa-Llah wa ashhadu anna Muhammadu Rasul-Allah—"I bear witness that there is no deity except Allah and I bear witness that Muhammad is Allah's messenger," the Islamic *Shahadah* or Declaration of Faith.

Astaghfirullah—I seek Allah's forgiveness.

A'udhu bil-Lahi min ash-Shaytani-r-Rajeem—I seek refuge in God from Satan the accursed.

Awliya (sing., **wali**)—the "friends" of Allah, Muslim saints or holy people.

Bayt al-Maqdis—the Sacred House in Jerusalem, built at the site where Solomon's Temple was later erected.

Barakah—blessings.

Batil—vain or false; falsehood, deception.

Bayah—pledge; in the context of this book, the pledge of a disciple (murid) to a sheikh.

Bi-hurmati-l-Fatehah—for the honor or respect of Surat al-Fatehah (the opening chapter of the Qur'an).

Bismillahi-r-Rahmani-r-Raheem—"In the name of Allah, the Beneficent, the Merciful," the invocation with which all a Muslim's actions are supposed to begin.

Dajjal—the False Messiah whom the Prophet ﷺ foretold as coming at the end-time of this world, who will deceive mankind with pretensions of being divine.

Day of Promises—the occasion in the spiritual world when Allah Almighty called together the souls of all human beings to come and asked them to acknowledge His Lordship and sovereignty (7:172).

Dhikr (zikr, zikir)—message, remembrance or reminder, used in the Qur'an to refer to the Qur'an and other revealed scriptures. Dhikr (or dhikr-Allah) also refers to remembering Allah through repetition of His Holy Names or various phrases of glorification (for the meanings of the phrases of dhikr mentioned in this book, see the footnote entries under individual phrases).

Du'a—supplication, personal prayer.

Dunya—this world and its attractions, worldly involvements.

Efendi—mister, sir.

'Eid—festival; the two major festivals of Islam are 'Eid al-Fitr, marking the completion of Ramadan, and 'Eid al-Adha, the Festival of Sacrifice during the time of Hajj.

Fard—obligatory, prescribed.

Fard al-kifayah – an obligation which suffices to be met by one or a few persons in a community.

Fatehah—al-Fatehah, the opening surah or chapter of the Qur'an.

Fitnah (pl., **fitan**)—trial, test, temptation; also, discord, dissension.

Grandshaykh—a wali of great stature. In this text, where spelled with a capital "G," "Grandshaykh" refers to Mawlana 'Abdullah ad-Daghestani, Shaykh Nazim's shaykh, to whom he was closely attached for forty years up to the time of Grandshaykh's death in 1973.

Hadith (pl., **ahadith**)—a report of the Holy Prophet's sayings, contained in the collections of early hadith scholars. In this text, "Hadith" has been used to refer to the entire body of his oral traditions, while "hadith" denotes an individual tradition.

Halal—lawful, permissible.

Hajji—one who has performed Hajj, the sacred pilgrimage of Islam.

Halal—permitted, lawful according to the Islamic Shari'ah.

Haqq—truth, reality.

Haram—forbidden, unlawful.

Hasha—God forbid! Never!

Haqq—truth, reality.

Haram—prohibited, unlawful.

Hasan al-Basri – a great scholar of the seventh century C.E.

Hawa—desires, lusts, passions of the lower self or nafs.

Hidayah/hidayat—guidance.

Hijab—barrier, screen, veil or curtain; the covering of Muslim women.

Himmah—desire, zeal, eagerness, ambition, determination.

Hu—the divine pronoun, He.

Ibrahim--the prophet Abraham.

Imam—leader; specifically, the leader of a congregational prayer.

Iman—faith, belief.

Iman—faith, belief.

Insha'Allah – God willing, if God wills.

'Isa—the prophet Jesus.

'Isha – night; specifically, the night prayer.

Jababirah—tyrants, oppressors.

Jinn—an invisible order of beings created by Allah from fire.

Kafir—a denier or rejector; in an Islamic context, one who denies Allah (an unbeliever or atheist) or does not acknowledge or is ungrateful for divine favors.

Khalifah—deputy, successor, vice-gerent.

Khidr—a holy man, mentioned in the Qur'an, 18:60-82, to whom God has granted life up to the end of the world..

Kufr—unbelief, denial of Allah.

La hawla wa la quwwata illa bil-Lah al-'Aliyi-l-'Azheem—"There is no might nor power except in Allah, the Most High, the All-Mighty," words that Muslims utter frequently during their daily lives, signifying total reliance upon Allah.

La ilaha illa-Llah, Muhammadu rasul-Allah—there is no deity except Allah, Muhammad is the Messenger of Allah.

Mahdi–the divinely-appointed guide whose coming at the end-time of this world is mentioned in several authoritative hadiths. He will lead the believers and establish a rule of justice and righteousness for a period of time prior to the events preceding the end of the world and the Last Judgment.

Masha'Allah—what or as Allah willed.

Masjid—literally, a place where sujud, prostration, is made, i.e., a mosque.

Mawla—master, lord, protector, patron, referring to Allah Most High.

Me'raj—the Holy Prophet's ascension to the Heavens and the Divine Presence.

Muezzin—one who makes the call to prayer (adhan).

Muluk (sing., **malik**)—kings, monarchs.

Mumin/muminah—male/female believers in Islam.

Munkar--that which is disapproved, rejected or considered abominable in Islam.

Murid—a disciple or follower of a shaykh.

Murshid—spiritual guide, pir.

Musa—the prophet Moses ﷺ.

Muwahhid – one who proclaims the Unity of Allah Almighty.

Nafs—(1) soul, self, person; (2) the lower self, the ego.

Nasihah—good advice or counsel, admonition, reminder.

Nur—light.

Qada wa qadar—the sixth pillar of Islamic faith, referring to the divine decree.

Qiblah—direction; specifically, the direction of Mecca.

Qisas—retaliation.

Qiyamat/Qiyamah—the Day of Resurrection.

Rabi'ah al-Adawiyah—Rabi'ah Basri, a great womansaint of the eighth century C.E.

Rabitah—bond, connection, tie, link, in the context of this book, with a shaykh.

Rak'at—a cycle or unit of the Islamic prayer (salat), which is repeated a specified number of times in each prayer.

Ramadan—the ninth month of the Islamic lunar calendar, the month of fasting.

Rasul-Allah—the Messenger of God, Muhammad ﷺ.

Sahabah (sing., sahabi)—the Companions of the Prophet, the first Muslims.

Sajdah (also sujud)—prostration.

Salat—the prescribed Islamic prayer or worship.

Sallallahu 'alayhi was-sallam—Islamic invocation on the Prophet ﷺ, meaning, "May Allah's peace and blessings be upon him."

Salawat—invoking blessings and peace upon the Holy Prophet ﷺ.

Sayyid—leader; also, a descendant of the Holy Prophet.

Sayyidina—our chief, master.

Sayyidina 'Ali—the cousin and son-in-law of the Prophet ﷺ and the fourth caliph of Islam.

Sayyidina 'Umar—'Umar ibn al-Khattab, the Prophet's eminent Companion and the second caliph of Islam.

Shahadah—the Islamic creed or Declaration of Faith, "Ash-shadu an la ilaha illa-Llah wa ashhadu anna Muhammu rasul Allah, I bear witness that there is no deity except Allah and I bear witness that Muhammad is His messenger."

Shah Naqshband—Grandshaykh Muhammad Bahauddin Shah-Naqshband, a great eighth century wali, the founder of the Naqshbandi Tariqah.

Shari'at/Shari'ah—the divine Law of Islam, based on the Qur'an and the Sunnah of the Prophet ﷺ.

Shirk—polytheism/idolatry, ascribing divinity or divine attributes to anything other than God.

Shaykh Sharafuddin—the shaykh of Grandshaykh 'Abdullah ad-Daghistani.

Shaytan—Satan.

Sohbet (Arabic, **suhbah**)—a shaykh's discourse (association).

Subhanallah—glory be to Allah.

Sultan al-Awliya—lit., "the king of the awliya,' the highest ranking saint.

Sunnah—the practice of the Holy Prophet; that is, what he did, said, recommended or approved of in his Companions. In this text, "Sunnah" is used to refer to the collective body of his actions, sayings or recommendations, while "sunnah" refers to an individual action or recommendation.

Surah—chapter of the Qur'an.

Takbeer—the pronouncement of God's greatness, "Allahu akbar, God is Most Great."

Taraweeh—the special nighly prayers of Ramadan.

Tariqah/tariqat—literally, way, road or path. An Islamic order or path of discipline and devotion under the guidance of a shaykh (*pir, wali*); Islamic Sufism.

Tawaf—the rite of circumambulatin the K'abah while glorifying Allah, one of the rites of Hajj and 'Umrah.

'Ulama (sing, **'alim**)—scholars, specifically of Islam.

'Umar—see Sayyidina **'Umar**.

Ummah—faith community, nation.

'Umrah—the minor pilgrimage to Mecca, which can be performed at any time of the year.

Uns—familiarity.

Wali (pl., **awliya**)—a Muslim holy man or saint.

Wa min Allah at-tawfeeq—And success is only from Allah.

Wudu—the prescribed minor ablution preceding prayers and other acts of worship.

Ya Rabb—O Lord.

Zakat/zakah—the obligatgory charity of Islam, one of its five "pillars" or acts of worship.

Zakat al-Fitr—the obligatory charity of 'Eid al-Fitr, the festival marking the completion of Ramadan.

Zhulm (**zulm**)—injustice, oppression, tyranny, misuse, transgressing proper limits, wrongdoing.

OTHER TITLES FROM
THE INSTITUTE FOR SPIRITUAL & CULTURAL ADVANCEMENT

Online ordering available from www.isn1.net

THE PATH TO SPIRITUAL EXCELLENCE
By Shaykh Muhammad Nazim Adil al-Haqqani
ISBN 1-930409-18-4, Paperback. 180 pp.

This compact volume provides practical steps to purify the heart and overcome the destructive characteristics that deprive us of peace and inner satisfaction. On this amazing journey doubt, fear, and other negative influences that plague our lives - and which we often pass on to our children - can be forever put aside. Simply by introducing in our daily lives those positive thought patterns and actions that attract divine support, we can reach spiritual levels that were previously inaccessible.

IN THE MYSTIC FOOTSTEPS OF SAINTS
By Shaykh Muhammad Nazim Adil al-Haqqani
Volume 1 - ISBN 1-930409-05-2
Volume 2 – ISBN 1-930409-09-5
Volume 3 – ISBN 1-930409-13-3, Paperback. Ave. length 200 pp.

Narrated in a charming, old-world storytelling style, this highly spiritual series offers several volumes of practical guidance on how to establish serenity and peace in daily life, heal emotional and spiritual scars, and discover the role we are each destined to play in the universal scheme.

CLASSICAL ISLAM & THE NAQSHBANDI SUFI TRADITION
By Shaykh Muhammad Hisham Kabbani
ISBN 1-930409-23-0, Hardback. 950 pp.
ISBN 1-930409-10-9, Paperback. 744 pp.

This esteemed work includes an unprecedented historical narrative of the forty saints of the renowned Naqshbandi Golden Chain, dating back to Prophet Muhammad in the early seventh century. With close personal ties to the most recent saints, the author has painstakingly compiled rare accounts of their miracles, disciplines, and how they have lent spiritual support throughout the world for fifteen centuries. Traditional Islam and the Naqshbandi Sufi Tradition is a shining tribute to developing human relations at the highest level, and the power of spirituality to uplift humanity from its lower nature to that of spiritual triumph.

GUIDEBOOK OF DAILY PRACTICES AND DEVOTIONS
By Shaykh Muhammad Hisham Kabbani
ISBN 1-930409-22-2, Paperback. 352 pp.

This book details the spiritual practices which have enabled devout seekers to awaken certainty of belief and to attain stations of nearness to the Divine Presence. This detailed compilation, in English, Arabic and transliteration, includes the daily personal dhikr as well as the rites performed with every obligatory prayer, rites for holy days and details of the pilgrimage to Mecca and the visit of Prophet Muhammad in Madinah.

NAQSHBANDI *AWRAD* OF SHAYKH NAZIM
Compiled by Shaykh Muhammad Hisham Kabbani
ISBN 1-930409-06-0, Paperback. 104 pp.

This book presents in detail, in both English, Arabic and transliteration, the daily, weekly and date-specific devotional rites of Naqshbandi practitioners, as prescribed by the world guide of the Naqshbandi-Haqqani Sufi Order, Mawlana Shaykh Muhammad Nazim Adil al-Haqqani.

PEARLS AND CORAL, I & II
By Shaykh Muhammad Hisham Kabbani
ISBN 1-930409-07-9, Paperback. 220 pp.
ISBN 1-930409-08-7, Paperback. 220 pp.

A series of lectures on the unique teachings of the Naqshbandi Order, originating in the Near East and Central Asia, which has been highly influential in determining the course of human history in these regions. Always pushing aspirants on the path of Gnosis to seek higher stations of nearness to the God, the Naqshbandi Masters of Wisdom melded practical methods with deep spiritual wisdom to build an unequalled methodology of ascension to the Divine Presence.

THE SUFI SCIENCE OF SELF-REALIZATION
By Shaykh Muhammad Hisham Kabbani
ISBN 1-930409-29-X, Paperback. 244 pp.

The path from submersion in the negative traits to the unveiling of these six powers is known as migration to Perfected Character. Through a ten-step program, the author--a master of the Naqshbandi Sufi Path--describes the science of eliminating the seventeen ruinous characteristics of the tyrannical ego, to achieve purification of the soul. The sincere seeker who follows these steps, with devotion and discipline, will acheive an unveiling of the six powers which lie dormant within every human heart.

ENCYCLOPEDIA OF ISLAMIC DOCTRINE
Shaykh Muhammad Hisham Kabbani
ISBN: 1-871031-86-9, Paperback, Vol. 1-7.

The most comprehensive treatise on Islamic belief in the English language. The only work of its kind in English, Shaykh Hisham Kabbani's seven volume Encyclopedia of Islamic Doctrine is a monumental work covering in great detail the subtle points of Islamic belief and practice. Based on the four canonical schools of thought, this is an excellent and vital resource to anyone seriously interested in spirituality. There is no doubt that in retrospect, this will be the most significant work of this age.

THE APPROACH OF ARMAGEDDON?
by Shaykh Muhammad Hisham Kabbani
ISBN 1-930409-20-6, Paperback 292 pp.

This unprecedented work is a "must read" for those interested in broadening their understanding of centuries-old religious traditions pertaining to the Last Days. This book chronicles scientific breakthroughs and world events of the Last Days as foretold by Prophet Muhammad. Also included are often concealed ancient predictions of Islam regarding the appearance of the anti-Christ, Armageddon, the leadership of believers by Mahdi ("the Savior"), the second coming of Jesus Christ, and the tribulations preceding the Day of Judgment. We are given final hope of a time on earth filled with peace, reconciliation, and prosperity; an age in which enmity and wars will end, while wealth is overflowing. No person shall be in need and the entire focus of life will be spirituality."

KEYS TO THE DIVINE KINGDOM
By Shaykh Muhammad Hisham Kabbani
ISBN 1-930409-28-1, Paperback. 140 pp.

God said, "We have created everything in pairs." This has to do with reality versus imitation. Our physical form here in this earthly life is only a reflection of our heavenly form. Like plastic fruit and real fruit, one is real, while the other is an imitation. This book looks at the nature of the physical world, the laws governing the universe and from this starting point, jumps into the realm of spiritual knowledge - Sufi teachings which must be "tasted" as opposed to read or spoken. It will serve to open up to the reader the mystical path of saints which takes human beings from the world of forms and senses to the world within the heart, the world of gnosis and spirituality - a world filled with wonders and blessings.

MY LITTLE LORE OF LIGHT
By Hajjah Amina Adil
ISBN 1-930409-35-4, Paperback, 204 pp.

A children's version of Hajjah Amina Adil's four volume work, *Lore Of Light*, this books relates the stories of God's prophets, from Adam to Muhammad, upon whom be peace, drawn from traditional Ottoman sources. This book is intended to be read aloud to young children and to be read by older children for themselves. The stories are shortened and simplified but not changed. The intention is to introduce young children to their prophets and to encourage thought and discussion in the family about the eternal wisdom these stories embody.

MUHAMMAD: THE MESSENGER OF ISLAM
By Hajjah Amina Adil
ISBN 1-930409-11-7, Paperback. 608 pp.

Since the 7th century, the sacred biography of Islam's Prophet Muhammad has shaped the perception of the religion and its place in world history. This book skilfully etches the personal portrait of a man of incomparable moral and spiritual stature, as seen through the eyes of Muslims around the world. Compiled from classical Ottoman Turkish sources and translated into English, this comprehensive biography is deeply rooted in the life example of its prophet.

www.ingramcontent.com/pod-product-compliance
Lightning Source LLC
Chambersburg PA
CBHW030311080526
44584CB00012B/523